Christian Ethics
and U.S. Foreign Policy

Christian Ethics and U.S. Foreign Policy

The Helsinki Accords and Human Rights

L. Larry Pullen

LEXINGTON BOOKS
Lanham • Boulder • New York • Oxford

LEXINGTON BOOKS

Published in the United States of America
by Lexington Books
4720 Boston Way, Lanham, Maryland 20706

12 Hid's Copse Road
Cumnor Hill, Oxford OX2 9JJ, England

British Library Cataloguing in Publication Information Available

Library of Congress Cataloging-in-Publication Data

Pullen, L. Larry, 1947-
    Christian ethics and U.S. foreign policy : the Helsinki accords and human rights / L.
Larry Pullen.
        p. cm.
    Includes bibliographical references and index.
    ISBN 0-7391-0110-2 (alk. paper)
    1. Human rights—Religious aspects—Christianity. 2. Conference on Security and
Cooperation in Europe (1972 : Helsinki, Finland) Final Act. 3. United States—Foreign
relations—Moral and ethical aspects. 4. Christianity and international affairs. 5.
Christian ethics. I. Title.

BT738.14 .P84 2000
241'.624—dc21   99-087954

Printed in the United States of America

♾™ The paper used in this publication meets the minimum requirements of American
National Standard for Information Sciences—Permanence of Paper for Printed Library
Materials, ANSI/NISO Z39.48–1992.

Dedicated to:

Kristy Arnesen Pullen and Margaret Pullen Bishop

Contents

Acknowledgments

In any book it seems there are many persons whose ideas either deliberately or otherwise seep into the fabric of the work. Several people in a very deliberate way have helped shape this book in its original form as a dissertation, and without whose help I would not have been able to write either the dissertation or this book. Among the readers of a very early draft was Robin Lovin. David Cowell and Don Jones both read several drafts and made invaluable suggestions. I was most fortunate to have Roger Lincoln Shinn read this over several times and make comments that improved it enormously. Lexington Books provided an anonymous reader who made suggestions, that while I did not incorporate them all, nevertheless improved the final work. Robin Adler, Lynn Weber, Serena Leigh and Dawn Stoltzfus of Roman and Littlefield all have provided support and instruction with the great patience and goodwill my writing style and I required. My technological backwardness was more than matched by Price Dempler's computer expertise without which this project would never have been completed. Of course, I alone am responsible for the final product; any shortcomings clearly rest with the author.

Grateful acknowledgment is given for permission to reprint the following copyrighted material: "Morality and U.S. Foreign Policy" by Charles Frankel in *Private and Public Ethics: Tensions Between*

Conscience and Institutional Responsibility, ed. Donald G. Jones. Copyright 1978 by The Edwin Mellen Press. Used by permission of The Edwin Mellen Press. Reprinted with the permission of Scribner, a Division of Simon & Schuster from *Moral Man and Immoral Society* by Reinhold Niebuhr. Copyright 1932 by Charles Scribner's Sons; copyright renewed © 1960 by Reinhold Niebuhr.

On a personal level I owe an enormous debt to the late Kenneth L. Smith of Colgate Rochester Divinity School-Bexley Hall-Crozer Theological Seminary for systematically introducing me to the work of Reinhold Niebuhr. My daughters, Nora and Abby, constantly remind me of what is important and why I search for the means to a more peaceful world. My sister, Margaret Pullen Bishop, and my wife, Kristy Arnesen Pullen, to whom this book is dedicated, have sustained me in so many ways that I can't begin to thank them enough.

Introduction

The book explores the influence of Christian ethics in the human rights provisions of the Helsinki Final Accord of the Conference on Security and Cooperation in Europe (CSCE). More broadly, it explores whether or not Christian realism may provide useful insights for foreign policy that is lacking in much actual practice. A Christian realist approach to international relations could provide an ethical facet that would promote human rights without ignoring other interests and values. Thus, Christian realism would have encouraged Dr. Kissinger (and President Nixon) to place greater emphasis on human rights early in the policy process, and would have restrained President Carter from placing imprudent emphasis on human rights in foreign policy.

The articulation of a Christian realist ethical perspective in regard to foreign policymaking will suggest an appropriate role for morality in international relations. In order to illuminate the strengths of Christian realism's ethical perspective, it will be compared to the perspective of conventional realism or realpolitik as well as to that of conventional moralism.

The preliminary work on the Helsinki Accord began in 1973 and thus is a logical starting point for this book. The study ends in 1980, the end of the Carter administration and the beginning of the Reagan administration. The Nixon (and Kissinger) era represented the dominance of realpolitik while the Carter years clearly reflected a more idealistic or conventionally moralistic approach to foreign policy. Thus across the span of three administrations (i.e., including the Ford administration) there developed two rather distinct approaches to foreign policy as well as two significantly different policies toward the Soviet Union both outside of and within the CSCE process.

While the study makes the case for Christian realism as distinct from moralism and realpolitik, it will be shown that the Christian realist approach can be articulated in a way that does not require or expect policymakers or a nation to be Christian. That is, the Christian element in this form of realism can be translated into the language that is accessible to all members of a pluralistic society. In a diverse, democratic society the legitimacy (in a constitutional sense) and the effectiveness (in terms of policy adoption and acceptance) of religiously based policy advocacy requires broad—based acceptance of both the language in which the argument is made and the content of the policy advocated.

The issue of the role of ethics in international relations is a concern of long standing for political scientists, public officials, and ethicists. It has found recent expression in the investigations of the political scientist Stanley Hoffmann[1] and the social ethicist Robert W. McElroy.[2] A book devoted to more specifically Christian ethics and U.S. foreign policy was written by John C. Bennett and Harvey Seifert.[3] Writing earlier, Reinhold Niebuhr was both systematic and cogent on this topic and, while in some ways his writings are dated, especially since the end of the Cold War, they remain relevant for our understanding of ethics and U.S. foreign policy. Two other works in the area of human rights that are important for the purposes of this study are Max Stackhouse's *Creeds, Society, and Human Rights: A Study in Three Cultures* and Jo Renee Formicola's dissertation, *The American Catholic Church and Its Role in the Formulation of United States Human Rights Foreign Policy 1945 - 1978.* Previous research on the Helsinki Accord has focused on the Accord itself or on its impact rather than on the issues of ethics and U.S. foreign policy. John J. Maresca, as one of the Accord's negotiators early in the process, offers insight into the dynamics of getting CSCE started in his book *To Helsinki: The Conference on Security and Cooperation in Europe 19731975.* The most extensive one-volume overview of the Helsinki process is William Korey's *The Promises We Keep: Human Rights, the Helsinki Process, and American Foreign Policy.*

Warren Lee Holleman, a medical ethicist, in his book *The Human Rights Movement: Western Values and Theological Perspectives* makes a case for a Christian realist approach to human rights. Like most scholars dealing with Christian realism, he refers primarily to the work of Reinhold Niebuhr. This book contributes to the study of Niebuhr's thought because Niebuhr himself does not directly address the concern for human rights. Rather Niebuhr explores the topic of human rights under other concepts such as freedom. In addition to Holleman's book, Robin Lovin's *Reinhold Niebuhr and Christian Realism* also addresses the implications of Christian realism for human rights.

Understanding how Christian realism approaches human rights, international relations, and the possibilities and limitations under which foreign policy is made and executed constitutes a significant part of this dissertation. The original contribution of this project lies in its juxtaposition of Christian realism with the historical data relating U.S. foreign policy and the CSCE in the period 1973-1980. In addition, original material on how mainline Protestant churches attempted to influence U.S. human rights policy in the CSCE process will be presented as a means of illuminating Christian realism. Reviewing Niebuhr's writing in this context will strike many, perhaps most, readers as novel because Niebuhr emphasized an anti-moralistic approach to foreign policy, and the promotion of human rights is almost always seen today as synonymous with morality in foreign policy. One task of this work is to demonstrate that Niebuhrian realism can reconcile the promotion of human rights with a prudent foreign policy.

In the academic community a revitalized appreciation for the potential contribution of a *Christian* realism may help generate theory and may help explain and guide foreign policymaking more adequately. In his book *Controversies in International Relations Theory: Realism and the Neoliberal Challenge*, Charles W. Kegley Jr. makes clear the need for just such a revitalization of theory-building. Kegley states that what is needed is not an "unrestrained re-embrace of realism alongside the repudiation of the new liberal approaches, but for a melding of the two."[4] From the perspective of a Christian ethicist it is hoped this study will encourage a re-examination of the contribution of Christian realism to political debate.

Methodologically this study will draw on the historical data surrounding U.S. foreign policymaking in relation to the Soviet Union and the CSCE. An analysis will be made of the considerations both domestic and foreign that led to the positions taken by the U.S. government. It will also analyze statements regarding human rights and the Helsinki Accord made by mainline Protestant denominations or organizations such as the National Council of Churches of Christ to determine the ethical perspectives of those churches. (The National Council of Churches of Christ is an agency of thirty-two Protestant, Episcopal, and Orthodox denominations.) As church statements and Christian realist writings are examined observations will be made about how these perspectives are presented to persuade members of a pluralistic society.

The dialectic that Christian realism holds in tension is between a too optimistic view of human nature and progress and a too pessimistic view of human nature and history. That dialectic will likely reveal the variety of goals a nation may be seeking in its foreign policy at any given moment. At the same time it is also possible that this study will show the weaknesses of using an ethical approach such as Christian realism, first because it is so concerned with consequences, which of themselves are so unpredictable. From the perspective of nongovernmental activists a more liberal Christian ethics might seem more useful. Because of its concern for all the details surrounding policymaking and its emphasis on the limits of what is possible in policymaking, Christian realism may seem more designed to aid policymakers rather than religiously inspired political activists who do not readily perceive the limits of what is possible, since they are not responsible for policymaking. This is not meant to suggest that policymakers are not religiously inspired political activists of a sort; it is meant to distinguish them from denominational or religious persons whose major concern is to bring a prophetic word to public policymaking. These non-policymakers are often driven by a vision that is utopian and arguably not particularly helpful within a given issue or context.

The terms *Christian realism* and *idealism* need to be defined or at least characterized. Within the body of the book a fuller description of each position will be developed. In an essay entitled "Augustine's Political Realism" Reinhold Niebuhr defines the terms when he writes:

The terms "idealism" and "realism" are not analogous in political and in metaphysical theory; and they are certainly not as precise in political, as in metaphysical, theory. In political and moral theory "realism" denotes the disposition to take all factors in a social and political situation, which offer resistance to established norms, into account, particularly the factors of self-interest and power. . . . "Idealism" is, in the esteem of its proponents, characterized by loyalty to moral norms and ideals, rather than to self-interest, whether individual or collective. It is, in the opinion of its critics, characterized by a disposition to ignore or be indifferent to the forces in human life which offer resistance to universally valid ideals and norms.[5]

These definitions coming from the perspective of a realist may not do justice to the idealist position. For the idealist, human nature is essentially good or altruistic.[6] While there are several important factors that contribute to a more complete understanding of the differences, at the heart is the anthropological distinction.

In order to illustrate the strength of certain ethical theory chapters are organized to move from the historical data and ethical theory to an integration of the two. The first chapter addresses the evolution of the CSCE process and the human rights provisions, as well as U.S. foreign policy. This chapter presents the factors that had to be considered in formulating specific policy. The second chapter relates ethics to foreign policy by describing Christian realism, realism, and idealism. While the discussion draws distinctions among the three approaches it illustrates as well how they are complementary. Chapter three deals with the positions of mainline Protestant churches toward human rights. This chapter reveals the concerns expressed by the churches and offers an explanation as to why those particular concerns are lifted up. Chapter four explores the issue of how Christian ethical positions are raised, and should be raised, in a pluralistic society. The chapter defines human rights and explores the sources of human rights in order to reveal among other things the acculturation of the religious message. The final chapter will bring the analysis of Christian realism developed in the preceding three chapters together with the data on U.S. policy described in chapter one. Thus this chapter presents the concrete ways in which Christian realism may have helped in formulating policy related to the CSCE.

Hopefully the reader will find that the entire work will show churches how to join in the foreign policy formation process faithfully and effectively. In addition it is hoped the book will illustrate to policymakers a method of ethical analysis that will enhance their ability to make just and prudent policy decisions.

Notes

1. Stanley Hoffmann, *Duties Beyond Borders: On the Limits and Possibilities of Ethical International Politics* (Syracuse, N.Y.: Syracuse University Press, 1988).

2. Robert W. McElroy, *Morality and American Foreign Policy: The Role of Ethics in International Affairs* (Princeton, N.J.: Princeton University Press, 1992).

3. John C. Bennett and Harvey Seifert, *U.S. Foreign Policy and Christian Ethics* (Philadelphia: The Westminster Press, 1977), 11.

4. Charles W. Kegley Jr., ed., *Controversies in International Relations Theory: Realism and the Neoliberal Challenge* (N.Y.: St. Martin's Press, 1995), 17.

5. Reinhold Niebuhr, *Christian Realism and Political Problems* (N.Y.: Charles Scribner's Sons, 1953), 11920.

6. Kegley, *Controversies in International Relations Theory*, 4.

Chapter 1

Formation and Evolution of the CSCE

The Conference on Security and Cooperation in Europe (CSCE) was established in 1973 as a conference among the nations of Europe, except Albania, plus the United States and Canada. These thirty-five nations on August 1, 1975, signed an agreement known as the Final Accord (also known as the Final Act). It was designed to establish a mode of operation among the signatories that would enhance peace and security among those nations.[1]

The conference and agreement represent the end of a long process of discussion among the nations and, in particular, between the two major superpowers. They represent as well the beginning of the ongoing process known as the Conference on Security and Cooperation in Europe (CSCE). The ongoing CSCE process was made up of review conferences, which were held to evaluate how effectively the signatories were complying with the terms of the agreement, and experts' meetings, which addressed certain technical matters. The follow-up meetings were a significant achievement of the Final Act because without them the accord would simply be a declaration, while with them the Final Act took on a semi-juridical and politically binding character.[2] In the time period under discussion in this dissertation the only review conference completed was the one at Belgrade (October 1977 to March 1978). The Madrid follow-up conference began in November 1980.

One of the more significant aspects of the evolution of the CSCE is that the impetus for holding a security conference on Europe came from the Soviet Union. As early as January 1954, the Soviet Union suggested holding a conference on European security in order to legitimate the post-World War II boundaries of Europe. The United States as well as West European nations were, to say the least, reluctant to agree to any conference that might even hint at legitimizing Soviet domination of Eastern Europe. The United States in this regard, for example, never accepted the Soviet annexation of the Baltic states of Latvia, Lithuania, and Estonia. Certainly the Federal Republic of Germany was not about to accept a permanent division of Germany. Nevertheless, the Soviet Union was able to have the conference it wanted beginning in 1973.[3] Why were the Soviets able to get in 1973 what they could not get in 1954? What factors now made such a conference possible? The following discussion takes up these questions.

Global Context

Several interrelated factors created the climate for the 1973 European security conference. Significant among those factors were the continuing U.S. involvement in the Vietnam War, the U.S. overtures to China, the establishment of détente between the United States and the Soviet Union, internal changes within the Soviet Union, and the West European desire for better relations with the Soviet Union. While the informal meetings to set up the conference took place in 1972, the roots of CSCE go back even farther.

The Cuban missile crisis of 1962 was the closest the superpowers ever came to nuclear war, and it represented a great turning point in Soviet-American relations.[4] A thaw in the Cold War came about as a result of the crisis. Significantly, Henry Kissinger (who would later be the National Security adviser to President Nixon and the secretary of state), though deeply shaken by the missile crisis, saw in the crisis a possibility that both superpowers had learned in a more profound way that both nations could be destroyed, and they might, therefore, modify their policies to be less confrontational.   Kissinger, who had believed before the missile crisis that the USSR was the world's leading "revolutionary" power, came to believe, by 1969, that a Soviet-American community of interests based on the common need to avoid nuclear war could serve as the basis of a partnership for a stable world order.[5] Thus there was in Henry Kissinger's thinking (and also in Richard Nixon's) a basis for détente. Yet before détente could be fully enacted, the United States had to extricate itself from the Vietnam War.

As will be seen in the theoretical discussion on Christian realism in a later chapter, this ability to recognize shared interests is a major concern for Reinhold Niebuhr. This commonality of interests, which Nixon and Kissinger experienced and expressed in their roles as policymakers, Niebuhr understood through his study of history, human nature, and ethics. Thus while Nixon and Kissinger are understood as realists (and not as Christian or Niebuhrian realists) in understanding the shared need to avoid nuclear war, they did not fall into the trap of which Niebuhr warned, i.e., defining one's national interest too narrowly. Richard Nixon became president in 1969 largely because the American people were looking for a way to end U.S. involvement in Vietnam. "By 1970 America's resolve on Vietnam was growing ever weaker, and the Soviet Union was getting credit for exactly the right character and amount of help to Hanoi and its friends."[6] In the context of American public turmoil over Vietnam, the Sino-Soviet split, and the possibility of détente, Nixon sought to end U.S. involvement in Vietnam. Yet he did so with a grave concern over what might be the reaction at home and abroad if the United States were to withdraw from Vietnam too abruptly. Nixon feared a right-wing reaction in the United States if he pulled the country out too quickly. He feared increased instability in the outside world if American allies felt they could not count on the United States or if the Communists saw America's defeat in Vietnam as a weakness to be exploited.[7] Vietnam would be an obstacle to improved relations between the United States and the Soviet Union. Because American public opinion had turned against continuing the Vietnam War, Nixon would be unable to get either Moscow or Beijing to pressure Hanoi to reach a political settlement.[8] President Nixon instructed Dr. Kissinger before visiting Moscow in early 1972 to tell the Soviet leaders no strategic arms agreement was possible as long as the Vietnam War was going on.[9] For Nixon, 1972 was a key year in ending the Vietnam War. In February he had gone to China, and in

October Kissinger claimed peace was "at hand."[10] The agreement ending U.S. participation did not come in 1972, but it was signed in 1973.

The ending of the Vietnam War allowed Nixon and Kissinger to pursue détente. As Robert Dallek put it,

> By ending the war in Vietnam, Nixon and Kissinger freed themselves to meet what they described as "a new era of international relations" with "a new approach to foreign policy." The postwar period, they said, was now over. The years of American military predominance, anticommunist nations' dependence on the United States, and a unified Communist bloc had passed. Instead, the world now faced a Soviet-American military balance of power and insistence by Western, Communist, and newly emerging states on independence from superpower control. Changing conditions abroad coupled with disillusionment over Vietnam shattered postwar American convictions about containment. In light of all this, Nixon and Kissinger urged the need for a new international order or structure of peace that would reduce Cold War tensions and create a fresh foreign policy consensus in the United States.[11]

If Vietnam preoccupied the American consciousness up to the signing of the Paris Peace Accord in 1973, it would continue to pervade the American subconscious as Kissinger and Nixon began to elaborate their policy of détente.

Certainly the U.S. rapprochement with China was meant not only to normalize relations with China but also to influence Soviet behavior, official U.S. statements to the contrary notwithstanding. Yet the U.S. role as balancer between the two Communist nations would require skilled statescraft. China's Premier Zhou Enlai urged the United States to take the lead in organizing an anti-Soviet coalition. He thought negotiating with the Soviets would lead to confusion since the USSR was inherently expansionist. Yet Kissinger knew that though it was better for the United States to "be closer to either Moscow or Peking than either was to the other," if the United States got too close to either the policy might fail (and lead to a Soviet attack on China).[12]

Détente was not only supposed to be a two-way street by which both superpowers benefited, but it was to be carried on at a number of levels. Not only were military tensions to be lessened but so too were trade restrictions. "Kissinger believed that the problem of disarmament was not disarmament at all, but rather forging détente between the Soviet Union and the United States. The linkage approach was absolutely basic to his conception of détente."[13] The policy rested on a realistic analysis of the risks of a more consistently confrontational policy. The potential benefits of détente were tangible (such as arms control and increased trade). For Kissinger, détente represented a policy by which the United States could avoid appeasement on the one hand and nuclear war on the other.

In retrospect Kissinger saw how the complexity of the policy of détente lost the support of the American people. "Deterrence ran up against liberal ideology and its emotional evocation of peace in the abstract; coexistence grated on the liturgical anti-Communism of the right. American idealism drove both groups to challenge us from different directions."[14] What Kissinger did not seem to foresee in his role as policymaker was the potential for the victory of the liberal democratic system over Soviet communism, and consequently he did not know what role the CSCE might play in the demise of the Soviet Union and empire.

Another factor besides the U.S. policy of détente, which by 1972 created the atmosphere for a European security conference, was the Western European desire for better relations with the Soviet Union. This desire was not only the result of the growth of Soviet power and the relative decline of American power[15] but also the result of Willy Brandt's policy of *Ostpolitik* begun in 1969.[16] In addition, the West Europeans were concerned that the bilateral relationship between the United States and the Soviet Union might undermine their own security, and thus they sought a wider dialogue with the Soviets (and East Europeans) in the context of a European security conference.[17]

These factors then made the conditions right for a European security conference: the U.S. attempt to end its involvement in the Vietnam War, U.S. rapprochement with China, the policy of détente with the Soviet Union, and the West European desire to better relations with the Soviet Union. Given these factors, by late 1972 the United States was willing to agree to a European security conference in the interest of détente, but the leadership role it would take in the CSCE negotiations would vary considerably within the time frame under consideration. In order to understand the changing U.S. role, let us turn to an analysis of U.S. public opinion.

U.S. Public Opinion

From at least 1968 and the Tet Offensive in Vietnam until the signing of the Paris Peace Accord in 1973 American public opinion on foreign policy was preoccupied with ending the Vietnam War. Whether or not the American people understood the subtleties of the Nixon-Kissinger grand strategy of détente and the triangular relationship between Washington, Beijing, and Moscow, it seems clear that a large segment of the American public wanted U.S. involvement in Vietnam to end.

The CSCE came to public attention when plans were announced that a summit level meeting to sign the Helsinki accord was being planned. "The press, Congress, and the public were caught by surprise at the new importance attached to the negotiations."[18] President Ford's scheduled attendance at the Helsinki signing ceremony, set for August 1, 1975, "became the focus of a large-scale anti-détente, anti-Soviet and anti-Helsinki public campaign. Mail to the White House ran 10 to 1 urging Ford not to go."[19] An important part of the U.S. press saw the Helsinki Final Act as either meaningless or as a betrayal of U.S. interests and the interests of the East Europeans.[20] Former diplomat George Ball saw the process as "Capitulation at Helsinki"; and William Safire wrote, "In case you hadn't heard, World War II will soon be coming to its official end. The Russians won."[21]

At the time of its signing, American public opinion was far from supportive of the Final Act. The reading the American public was giving the accord was similar to the reading given it by the leadership of the Soviet Union; but given the different perspectives of each, the response to the document was quite different. In fact conservative presidential aspirants in the United States, both Gov. Ronald Reagan and Sen. Henry M. Jackson, spoke out against President Ford's participation in the signing ceremonies.[22] At the time the Final Act may have seemed just one more success for Soviet communism to an American public unhappy about the U.S. role in Vietnam and upset with the collapse of South Vietnam. In retrospect the demise of the Soviet Union and the credit given by East European human rights activists to the entire CSCE process in promoting human rights indicate how wrong American public opinion was about the Final Act.

As William Korey (an observer as well as a participant in CSCE follow-up conferences) has stated, Kissinger had reasons for downplaying the Final Act.

> Reasons for the downplaying varied. Kissinger had never been enthusiastic about the Helsinki process, and saw U.S. diplomacy related to the process largely as "damage control." Secondly, détente, of which the Helsinki accord was a quintessential expression, had appeared to have run its course. The fall of Saigon and the collapse of the South Vietnam regime brought bitterness and confusion in their wake. A communist victory in Asia was seemingly compounded by the threat of a possible communist takeover of Portugal in Western Europe. The very word "détente" was taboo in administration circles. Finally, lest excessive expectations about the Helsinki accord be raised publicly, official Washington thought the less said the better.[23]

At least initially, the concern that the public might have excessively high expectations about what might be accomplished via the Helsinki accord did not seem warranted. Human rights documents, including the relevant sections of the Final Act, would give the people of the United States an opportunity to express their idealism in their foreign policy. This obviously was a cause of concern for Kissinger, while it was a source of support for President Carter during his campaign and administration.

In Kissinger's judgment it was a serious mistake to try to influence Soviet practice in domestic matters. He believed that outside of the context of international diplomacy, linkage, if misapplied to internal policies, would set back détente as well as be counterproductive (as seen in the area of Jewish emigration).[24] Yet this certainly was not President Carter's view and, given the success of his campaign for the presidency, evidently not the view of the people who voted for President Carter.

"In its early weeks the Carter human rights policy aimed just as strongly at the Soviet bloc as at rightist governments. But as time passed the focus came to rest much more heavily on the latter."[25] Early on President Carter and spokespersons for the State Department spoke about the ideological initiative that promoting human rights would give and specifically identified the government of Czechoslovakia as violating the Helsinki accord in arresting and harassing Czech dissidents.[26]

These actions reflected not only President Carter's personal
commitment to human rights but also a concern, which campaign polls
had shown, that united liberals and conservatives. "Carter's human rights
theme served not only to draw support from various disparate
constituencies, it also served to tie together a variety of criticisms of the
incumbent."[27] Kissinger dates the liberal interest in human rights (as an
issue with which to criticize administration policy) as early 1973.

> Suddenly it was the liberal community that began to find ideological
> flaws in the détente that for so long it had passionately championed.
> The argument gained currency that Nixon "oversold" détente; that he
> neglected human rights in his desire to get along with the Kremlin; that
> the Administration was insensitive to the moral problem of dealing
> with Communism.[28]

While this criticism came naturally from the conservatives, it was more
difficult to hear from the other end of the political spectrum, even though
Kissinger was forced to admit: "The subtlest critique of our policy held
that our emphasis on the national interest ran counter to American
idealism and national character."[29] Whether the idealism has its roots in
the political left or political right, it is difficult to imagine sustaining any
foreign policy for a long period of time without drawing on that idealism.
Kissinger in the above quotation seems to be saying that it is the task of
political leadership to identify the national interest with American idealism
and the national character. Thus human rights became a centerpiece in
public opinion about U.S. foreign policy from the end of President
Nixon's first term, even if the human rights provisions of the Helsinki
Final Act did not stand out as significant at the time of the signing in
1975.

While U.S. public opinion was important in the evolving Helsinki
process and in defining the leadership role the United States would take in
it, public opinion was not the only factor in defining either the Final Act
or the subsequent follow-up conferences. It is to the specific context of the
Final Act and follow-up conferences that we now turn.

Context of the CSCE

While it is appropriate to look at the executive branch of government for leadership in the foreign policy realm, in the development of the Helsinki process over the period from 1973 to 1980 two significant groups of people not related to the executive branch of government made an important contribution to the CSCE. In the United States the Congress, responding in part to public opinion, argued for a higher profile for human rights in U.S. foreign policy. Soviet and East European dissidents, by monitoring Soviet compliance with the accord's human rights provisions through Helsinki Watch Groups, contributed significantly to the effectiveness of the Final Act. The Helsinki Watch Groups often contacted the U.S. Commission.

As early as 1974 the U.S. House of Representatives issued a report, based on hearings held August 1, 1973, to December 7, 1973, entitled *Human Rights in the World Community: A Call for U.S. Leadership*, which made recommendations as to how U.S. foreign policy could promote human rights. Included in the recommendations were the positions that the State Department should treat human rights factors as a regular part of foreign policy decision-making, should prepare human rights impact statements for all policies with significant human rights implications, and should respond to human rights practices without regard to whether the government is friendly, neutral, or unfriendly.[30] The report states explicitly:

> The Department of State should upgrade the consideration given to human rights in determining Soviet-American relations. While pursuing the objectives of détente, the United States should be forthright in denouncing Soviet violations of human rights and should raise the priority of the human rights factor particularly with regard to policy decisions not directly related to national security.[31]

Obviously the report's drafters attempted to avoid linking security issues and human rights too directly. In so doing the subcommittee was attempting both to have détente and promote human rights. A subsequent congressional review credited the report with stimulating organizational changes at the State Department.[32]

Of all the congressional input into the development of U.S. human rights policy, none was more significant with regard to Eastern Europe than the creation of a Commission on Security and Cooperation in Europe. As Rep. Dante Fascell stated:

> Private groups in the West, responding to the muffled voices of dissent and interested in promoting individual rights in Communist societies, and parliamentary leaders—especially in countries where international human rights were becoming a détente-related electoral issue—began to seek ways to ensure that the Soviet Union and other Eastern bloc states would not simply discard the promises made at Helsinki. In the United States, the concern of private groups and of a number of members of Congress resulted in the creation, in June 1976, of a new governmental body, the Commission on Security and Cooperation in Europe, known now as the Helsinki Commission.[33]

This body was composed of six representatives, six senators, and three executive branch officials (one each from the Departments of State, Defense, and Commerce).[34] As might be expected with such a bureaucratically diverse group, it has not been immune to political challenges in Washington. President Ford found it politically impossible to scuttle the Commission, given the challenge he was facing from Ronald Reagan for the presidential nomination and later the challenge he faced from Jimmy Carter (especially in light of Ford's gaffe that the Poles did not consider themselves dominated by the U.S.S.R. in the presidential debate).[35] State Department reluctance about the commission was altered by the election of President Carter with his emphasis on human rights, and both House and Senate foreign affairs committees thought a commission necessary to assure that both United States policy and public discussion would give appropriate emphasis to the human rights provisions of the Final Act.[36]

By the time the Belgrade review conference opened on October 4, 1977, the Helsinki Commission had become a major focal point for communication from Helsinki Watch Groups (most significantly the Moscow Group).[37] All of the members of the Helsinki Commission were members of the U.S. delegation (headed by former Supreme Court Justice Arthur Goldberg) to the Belgrade conference.[38] The status of the commission and the delegation as a whole portended well for the role the United States would take on at Belgrade. The United States took the lead in questioning East European countries about human rights, and in particular protested the repressive action by the Soviet government against Yuri Orlov, Anatoly Sharansky, and Aleksandr Ginsburg for their activities in the Moscow Helsinki Watch Group.[39]

As significant as the Helsinki Commission was as an organization for information on violations of the Final Act, it was Helsinki Watch groups in Eastern Europe that provided the data upon which the West was able to build its case against the Soviet Union. As Ludmilla Alexeyeva, a founding member of the Moscow Group, has written:

> In the late sixties it had seemed, and the KGB leadership supposed, that the human rights movement was finished. It is otherwise impossible to explain why the government took the unusual step in August 1975, of publishing in newspapers the complete text of the Final Act . . . including the humanitarian articles. It is possible that the Soviet leadership was in this instance overcome by a desire to boast to its own people of its success in Helsinki. . . . By the terms of the Final Act the Soviet Union received some substantial benefits; most important of these was recognition of the post World War II boundaries in Europe in exchange for the promise to observe human rights. Neither the Soviet leaders nor their Western counterparts had counted on substantial changes in Soviet internal politics. The commonly held opinion was that the humanitarian articles of the Final Act were nothing more than a joint gesture by the signing governments in deference to public opinion in democratic countries.[40]

When the Soviet government published the text of the Final Act, Soviet citizens became aware for the first time of the human rights obligations their government was under, and the people began appealing to the accords in their grievances to the government.[41] The dissident Yuri Orlov saw in the accords a means for promoting dialogue between the government and society and thereby for liberalizing the regime.[42] Even though some thought the human rights provisions of the Final Act were regressive in comparison with the Universal Declaration of Human

Rights, Orlov and ten others founded the Moscow Helsinki Watch Group on May 12, 1976, with the purpose of accepting information on violations of the humanitarian articles of the Final Act from citizens, compiling documents, and familiarizing the public and signatory governments with the contents of the documents.[43] Other similar groups were established in Ukraine, Lithuania, Georgia, and Armenia. These groups were composed of members of national movements in the corresponding areas.[44] The collection of material, particularly by the Moscow Group, had the effect of bringing together under one umbrella organization the complaints of a wide variety of dissidents in Soviet society.[45]

Similar groups were established in other East European countries. Each had the effect of animating public opinion and legitimating action for broader recognition of human rights. The leaders of these movements seemed to recognize that "(T)he natural allies of the human rights movement were the publics of the countries of the free world since their moral values coincided with the traditional values of Western democracies. . . ."[46]

The popular interest in CSCE both in the USSR and in the United States (as manifested in the Helsinki Commission) was the result of the development of the Final Act. In fact both the Watch groups and the commission played important roles, in part because the Final Act included provision for follow-up conferences. The process of holding the compliance conferences was lengthy and complex. During the period from late 1972 (when the preparatory talks began) to the end of 1980 (when the Madrid review conference began) the U.S. leadership role changed significantly.

Former Assistant Secretary of State for European Affairs, Arthur A. Hartman, in testimony before the Subcommittee on International Political and Military Affairs of the House Committee on International Relations, summarized the evolution of CSCE in May prior to signing the Final Act as follows:

> CSCE should be seen in perspective as but one aspect of our continuing efforts to move from confrontation to negotiation in strengthening East-West relations in Europe. The Soviet Union first proposed a European security conference in 1954 and periodically reiterated the proposal over subsequent years, but the Western and neutral nations showed

little enthusiasm for it. It appeared that Moscow's principle objective was to exploit such an event as a quasi-peace conference to produce a surrogate World War II peace treaty. In 1969, however, as nations of both East and West began to take increased bilateral initiatives toward détente, a renewed Warsaw Pact appeal for a European security conference elicited a cautiously positive reaction by NATO allies, who took the position that such a conference might serve a useful purpose after concrete progress had been achieved on the most sensitive aspect of East-West confrontation; namely, Berlin.[47]

A major obstacle to a European security conference, as Mr. Hartman's testimony points out, was the status of Berlin and, indeed, the status of the relationship between the German Democratic Republic (East Germany) and the Federal Republic of Germany (West Germany). In September 1971 the Berlin accord, which improved relations between people on both sides of the Berlin Wall, was signed, and it went into effect in June 1972. Having removed the major obstacle to the CSCE, multilateral preparatory talks began in Helsinki in November 1972.[48] Additionally, West German treaties with the Soviet Union and Poland, settling territorial disputes created by World War II, were ratified in May and became effective in June 1972 (a stated precondition for beginning CSCE).[49] In addition to the major obstacle of what a European security conference might mean for Berlin and Germany, the U.S. government worked to reassure the Baltic states—Latvia, Lithuania, and Estonia—that CSCE would not represent a reversal of the U.S. policy of non-recognition of their 1940 annexation by the Soviet Union.[50]

Kissinger and President Nixon wanted to begin talks with the Soviets on mutual and balanced force reductions (MBFR) in Europe. (The MBFR talks dealt exclusively with conventional weapons.) Consequently, Kissinger, during his visit to Moscow in September 1972, linked U.S. acceptance of the opening date of CSCE to Soviet acceptance of the opening of MBFR talks and the Soviets accepted.[51] Thus the United States accepted the Finnish invitation to begin the CSCE talks on November 22, and the preparatory MBFR discussions began in January 1973 in Vienna.[52]

As mentioned above, the U.S. position on CSCE, and in particular on the human rights provisions of the Final Act, changed over the course of the years from 1972 to 1980. It was not simply because of change in administrations that the United States took a more vocal position in promoting human rights. "The evolution in the U.S. approach was not part of a U.S. strategy. . . . Rather, the U.S. role responded to changing political pressures and needs, which in fact often determine the U.S. attitude in negotiations."[53] In fact, though Kissinger, as noted, was not predisposed to promote human rights or CSCE very vigorously, he significantly influenced the conference in securing two provisions: First, in bilateral U.S.-U.S.S.R. negotiations he arranged that future peaceful changes in frontiers be allowed in the Final Act so that West Germany could sign; second, he made it clear to the Soviet Union's leaders that they would have to grant further human rights concessions if the West was to accept the final conference results and go to Helsinki.[54] As U.S.-Soviet relations deteriorated in late 1974 and early 1975, Kissinger was more inclined to be firm with Moscow; and this attitude was increasingly evident in the CSCE toward the end of the negotiations.[55] Yet even so on balance the U.S. position was characterized by a "low profile," and it was the West Europeans, especially the British, who persisted in leading the fight for the human rights provisions of the Final Act.[56] At the early stages of the CSCE the United States was content to let its West European allies take the lead in promoting human rights.

The "low profile" was in keeping with the Nixon-Kissinger desire to make progress in bilateral negotiations with the Soviet Union over a wide range of issues. The growing public and congressional criticism of Kissinger's pragmatic realpolitik, the institutionalization of some of that criticism in the Helsinki Commission (created in large measure through the efforts of Sen. Claiborne Pell, Rep. Millicent Fenwick, and Rep. Dante Fascell), the activities of various Helsinki Watch groups, and the election of Jimmy Carter to the presidency all made an impact on the role the United States would take in CSCE.[57]

During the presidential campaign against Gerald Ford, Jimmy Carter not only picked up on Ford's debate blunder (when Ford suggested that the Poles did not consider themselves dominated by the USSR), but he also criticized President Ford for refusing to meet with exiled Soviet novelist Alexander Solzhenitsyn. In addition Carter accused President Ford of accepting the "so called doctrine of State Department official Helmut Sonnenfeldt that the United States should recognize a natural

Soviet sphere of influence in Eastern Europe."[58] As John Stoessinger put it:

> Carter found Kissinger's approach somewhat foreign to the American tradition. Americans, he believed, needed a measure of idealism in their foreign policy. The United States was different from other countries. It had once been a moral beacon light to others. It should be so again, despite Vietnam and despite Watergate. Kissinger had "Europeanized" American foreign policy and made it almost indistinguishable from the chessboard politics of power. What was needed now was an infusion of morality and ethics. In his debates with Gerald Ford, Carter emphasized that the Soviet Union, by signing the Helsinki Accords of 1975, had promised to observe the human rights of its citizens. A new concern with human rights would become the centerpiece of Carter's foreign policy. America would once again be "a city on a hill." Like its president, the nation's foreign policy, too, would have to be cleansed and born again.[59]

After Carter assumed the presidency in 1977 he welcomed Soviet dissident Vladimir Bukovsky to the White House, wrote a letter to the human rights activist Andrei Sakharov, and raised the case of Anatoly Sharansky (who had been accused of spying for the CIA) with Soviet Foreign Minister Andrei Gromyko.[60]

The Soviet Union's reaction to the Carter human rights policy was hostile and immediate. After President Carter had sent a letter of support to Andrei Sakharov, Secretary of State Cyrus Vance traveled to Moscow to seek a nuclear arms reduction agreement (March 1977). Instead of a successful discussion on arms reduction, Vance was lectured by Brezhnev on human rights abuses in the United States.[61] Of course the point of Brezhnev's lecture was to show how much the United States would dislike having its internal human rights policy aired in an international arena. President Carter had hoped to reject linkage of human rights to other elements in the U.S.-U.S.S.R. relationship when, in a speech at the United Nations (March 17, 1977), he said the administration "would protest Soviet misbehavior, such as violations of the Helsinki Accords, but it would not make any other aspect of U.S.-Soviet relations conditional on improvements in Soviet behavior."[62] Yet it was clear the Soviets were more than willing to link progress on SALT II (the Strategic Arms

Limitation Talks) with U.S. pronouncements on human rights in the Soviet sphere of influence.

In spite of the strong human rights position taken by the United States at the Belgrade review conference (October 1977-March 1978) "from the time of the March 1977 Vance mission to Moscow, the Carter administration pulled back from outspoken criticism of Soviet human rights violations."[63] The Carter administration learned that pursuing détente (a word not used for obvious reasons but a reality to be pursued nevertheless) and a vigorous pro-human rights foreign policy might not be compatible, especially if the human rights policy was high profile. In a speech at the University of Georgia Law School (April 1977), Secretary of State Vance took note of the dilemma when he said, "A sure formula for defeat of our goals would be a rigid, hubristic attempt to impose our values on others. A doctrinaire plan of action would be as damaging as indifference."[64] The United States had to be pragmatic in working for observance of human rights, for we must ask as Secretary Vance went on to say in the same speech, "Have we been sensitive to genuine security interests, realizing the outbreak of armed conflict or terrorism could in itself pose a serious threat to human rights?"[65] The president, because of the reality of this dilemma, was forced to prioritize between détente and human rights in a way that had not seemed clear to him before, and he shifted his concern to some extent away from human rights and toward détente.

Even if the Carter administration became more restrained after the Vance trip to Moscow in the spring of 1977, it did take a more active leadership role on human rights in the CSCE process than had previous administrations. On June 15, 1977, the preparatory meeting opened for the Belgrade review conference, and "[T]he United States, which had taken a back seat during most of the negotiating phase of the Final Act, now emerged as a leader in preparing for the Belgrade conference."[66] The Belgrade conference was to prove to be important not so much because of any diplomatic pronouncement resulting from the conference but because of the nature of the process developed by U.S. policy.

On October 18, 1977, a new U.S. policy made its debut in the Basket III (Cooperation in Humanitarian and Other Fields) Working Group. The head of the U.S. delegation, Arthur Goldberg, cited a United Press International story quoting a respectable Communist source about a trial of four supporters of the Charter 77 Human Rights Movement in Prague.[67] "What, heretofore, was always indirect, oblique, hazy, and vague was now unveiled. . . . The impact was stunning. The apparent sundering of the tacit understanding about specific incidents evoked an explosive response."[68] The four people had only wanted to talk to the Czechoslovak government about the Final Act, and now their cause was specifically cited in a way unknown in East-West diplomacy. The Soviet Union reacted strongly against the specific citation by Goldberg, and even the U.S. ally, Great Britain, through its foreign secretary, argued that human rights was only one element of the "complex web" of East-West relations.[69] Nevertheless, this 180 degree turn in U.S. policy led Max Kampelman, the subsequent head of the U.S. delegation to the Madrid (1980) review conference, to write, "historians may well say the shift of emphasis from détente to human rights began in Belgrade."[70] Despite the citation of specific cases, the Soviet Union and its allies refused to discuss the merits of any specific cases.[71] Rep. Dante Fascell, nevertheless, credits the conference with forcing some countries to ease repressive or restrictive practices, citing that some political prisoners were amnestied, families reunified, emigration rose, more bi-national marriages permitted, and some Western journals and newspapers began to appear in certain East European capitals.[72]

The operative assumption among the members of the Moscow Helsinki Watch Group was that international attention would lead to a lessening of repression within the USSR While this assumption may be valid in some instances, during and after the Belgrade conference the members of the Moscow Group experienced increased repression, with arrests and harsh sentences being given.[73] It should be noted that the Moscow Helsinki Watch Group prepared twenty-six documents for Belgrade; and, in spite of the group's experience of repression attending Belgrade, it prepared 138 documents for the Madrid conference in November 1980.[74]

The short document that resulted from the Belgrade conference did not refer to human rights. This Belgrade report merely stated that the signatory states reviewed the record of Final Act implementation and disagreed over how much progress had been made. It was agreed that another review conference would be held in Madrid in the fall of 1980. The Soviets felt as if they had won in that there was no more specific statement on human rights implementation.[75] Belgrade accomplished two things of consequence: "It established the human rights issue as a legitimate element of East-West diplomacy, and it provided for the continuation of the Helsinki process, which has . . . brought some progress in the human rights field."[76]

If, as Max Kampelman suggested, the Belgrade conference represented, in terms of U.S. foreign policy, a shift from an emphasis on détente to an emphasis on human rights, then the Madrid review conference, which began in 1980 elaborated even more fully a concern for human rights. Max Kampelman was named the head of the U.S. delegation by President Carter, a position he retained during the Reagan administration. Kampelman's championing of human rights extended enormously the process of mentioning names and cases.[77] "Kampelman transformed the Helsinki process, which had no formal implementing organ (just as it had no institutional apparatus), into a kind of mechanism of compliance."[78] Kampelman, ironically, belonged to the group of Democrats, led by Sen. Henry Jackson, who opposed President Ford's signing of the Final Act, and it was his tough anti-communism which made him attractive to President Carter's national security adviser, Zbigniew Brzezinski, and caused Brzezinski to recommend Kampelman to the president.[79]

The Helsinki process helped to expose the human rights violations in the Soviet Union and Eastern Europe in large part through the work of the Belgrade (October 1977 to March 1978) and Madrid (November 1980 to September 1983) follow-up conferences. The Helsinki Watch groups helped to animate human rights activities. The traditional Soviet position had been that, as a rule of international law, human rights issues were in the area of domestic jurisdiction and, therefore, not subject to international scrutiny. Eventually the Soviet Union, under domestic and international pressure, moved away from this position.

In writing or reading an essay on U.S.-Soviet relations, one should be cautious about attributing too much credit to any one factor in determining subsequent events. Thus, there were several events that influenced U.S.-Soviet relations both during and after the Carter administration. While it is beyond the scope of this study to do more than mention these occurrences, the reader should keep them in mind so as not to overemphasize the role of CSCE in the democratization process in the

Soviet Union. These occurrences were: (1) the Soviet deployment of SS20 missiles, which provided justification for the U.S. deployment of Cruise and Pershing II missiles in Europe; (2) the fall of the Shah of Iran and subsequent takeover of the U.S. embassy; (3) the Soviet invasion of Afghanistan;[80] and (4) the gradual decline of the economy of the Soviet Union. Now that the context for the CSCE, the Final Act, and the first two follow-up conferences has been described, let us examine in more detail the Final Act itself.

The Nature of the Helsinki Final Act

The Final Act of the Conference on Security and Cooperation in Europe, signed by thirty-five heads of government on August 1, 1975, was a very unusual document. It was unusual in the number of problems it dealt with, the diverse nature of the principles it expounded, the multitude of rules it stated, and the programs it formulated.[81] The Final Accord was given a great deal of political status as attested to by its signing at a summit meeting, but it was not given the legal standing of a treaty. The document itself did not initially epitomize the values it came to represent.

The Helsinki Final Act was a document written in informal, non-legislative language at the culmination of a two-year, three-stage process. Stage I negotiations, held in Helsinki ran from July 3 through July 7, 1973, ratified the Final Recommendations of the Helsinki Consultation (commonly referred to as the "Blue Book"), which laid the groundwork for the next three years of talks. Stage II negotiations (September 18, 1973, to July 21, 1975) in Geneva saw the work divided into three categories or "baskets." Stage III was the July 30, 1975, to August 1, 1975 final session where the Final Accord was signed.[82] This three-stage process, even though it was dealing with "European security," took into account the European-related roles of Canada and the United States by including them in the negotiations.

The first of the three baskets deals with "Questions Relating to Security in Europe." Included in Basket One is a "Declaration of Principles Guiding Relations between Participating States." The document describes ten principles which include: sovereign equality, respect for the rights inherent in sovereignty; refraining from the threat or use of force; inviolability of frontiers; territorial integrity of states; peaceful settlement

of disputes; nonintervention in internal affairs; respect for human rights
and fundamental freedoms, including the freedom of thought, conscience,
religion or belief; equal rights and self-determination of peoples;
cooperation among states; and fulfillment in good faith of obligations
under international law. It is here in the declaration of principles that
human rights is stated in a most general but significant fashion (a subject
to which we will return), but it is also here that the status quo is protected
by descriptions of respect for the rights inherent in sovereignty and
nonintervention in a state's internal affairs. In addition to setting out the
principles outlined above, the first basket provides a "Document on
Confidence-Building Measures and Certain Aspects of Security and
Disarmament."[83]

Basket II deals with "Cooperation in the Field of Economics, of
Science and Technology and of the Environment." Within this part of the
document provisions are made for commercial exchanges, industrial
cooperation and projects of common interest, trade and industrial
cooperation, science and technology, the environment and other areas
(transport, tourism, and migrant labor).[84]

Finally, the famous Basket III addresses "Cooperation in
Humanitarian and Other Fields." Along with Part VII ("Respect for
Human Rights and Fundamental Freedoms, Including Freedom of
Thought, Conscience, Religion or Belief") of the principles in Basket I,
Basket III contains the human rights provisions of the Helsinki Final Act.
The introductory paragraphs state:

> The participating States, Desiring to contribute to the strengthening of
> peace and understanding among peoples and to the spiritual
> enrichment of the human personality without distinction as to race, sex,
> language or religion, Conscious that increased cultural and educational
> exchanges, broader dissemination of information, Contacts between
> people, and the solution of humanitarian problems will contribute to the
> attainment of these aims, Determined   therefore to cooperate among
> themselves, irrespective of their political, economic and social systems,
> in order to create better conditions in the above fields, to develop and
> strengthen existing forms of cooperation and to work out new ways and
> means appropriate to these aims, Convinced that this cooperation
> should take place in full respect for the principles guiding relations

among participating States as set forth in the relevant document, Have adopted the following . . .[85]

The basket then goes on to elaborate on human contacts, information, cooperation and exchanges in the field of culture, and cooperation and exchanges in the field of education. Within the section on human contacts there are eight subheadings; and among these there are four that deserve special attention: "Contacts and Regular Meetings on the Basis of Family Ties," "Reunification of Families," "Marriage between Citizens of Different States," and "Travel for Personal and Professional Reasons."[86] These four areas were fields especially susceptible, according to Rep. Fascell, to the pressures of the Belgrade review conference. Given Germany's divided status at the time, the provisions were also significant for its population.

Specifically Basket III's information section committed participating states to, among other things, "favour increased cooperation among mass media organizations, including press agencies, as well as among publishing houses and organizations;" and "encourage meetings and contacts both between journalists' organizations and between journalists from the participating States. . . ."[87] These are the types of Basket III provisions that would become contentious.

The Final Act, as stated earlier, makes provision for periodic follow-up conferences. As noted in discussing the Belgrade conference, by providing for follow-up conferences the CSCE was able to promote compliance with the human rights provisions. These follow-up conferences served to legitimate international examination of the participating states' human rights practices. Even so, the Final Act was anything but self-executing.

Even though Basket III is known as the human rights portion of the Final Act, in some ways the principles provision of Basket I really provides more support for human rights in general.[88] It may be argued whether general human rights provisions are less significant or more significant in promoting human rights compliance than those more specific provisions. In either case, in the words of one international legal expert, "The defects of the human rights provisions of the Final Act are evident— they do not express binding legal commitments, and they are too general."[89] And in this context the international lawyer was writing about both Basket I and Basket III provisions. Even so, the Helsinki Final Act's human rights stipulations are more specific, more detailed, and less far reaching than United Nations documents dealing with human rights.[90]

It is one of the characteristics of international law, or law in general, that the importance of legal provisions cannot be separated from the political and/or public will behind them. "The term 'Final Act of a diplomatic conference' in practice covers instruments that vary in effect according to the circumstances."[91] Certainly subsequent events illustrate just how circumstances made the human rights segments of the Final Act significant. From the signing it was clear that, for whatever reasons, the participating states placed great significance on the document.

> Having deliberately ruled out the adoption of a treaty, the participating states wanted to bring to light, in the most solemn way, the importance which they attributed to the results of their work: the terms of the Final Act itself, and particularly its preamble, show the importance and the extent of the undertaking. The gathering of the heads of state and government at Helsinki for the signing ceremony which recalls the great landmarks of world diplomacy, bears witness to this. But even more significant is the entirely novel provision pursuant to which "the text of this Final Act will be published in each participating State, which will disseminate it and make it known as widely as possible."[92]

The sentence requiring the publication of the Final Act is in keeping with the principle stipulated in Part VII of Basket I, that each individual has the right to know his or her rights under the Final Act.

In the realm of the development of international law, the Final Act was in the nebulous area of norm development. Thus, as has been stated, the Final Act was not a treaty and thus did not create legally binding obligations, but "it was strongly emphasized (at the conference), however, that this conclusion should not detract from the great legal significance of the Helsinki Final Act."[93] As Thomas Buergenthal writes:

> The following considerations, *inter alia*, were deemed by the conference participants to explain or relate to the legal significance of this instrument: 1. As an agreement among states, notwithstanding the fact that it is not legally binding, the Helsinki Final Act must be interpreted by reference to relevant principles of international law. . . .

2. Without being legally binding, the Helsinki Final Act establishes a valid basis, as between the signatory states, for seeking information and exchanging views on the Helsinki Final Act, for making demands for compliance with its provisions and for monitoring such compliance. That is to say, although a signatory state's failure to comply with these demands does not give rise to a legal claim or legal remedies for nonperformance, the Act legitimates appropriate peaceful political action to obtain performance. 3. By incorporating and invoking preexisting principles of international law, the Helsinki Final Act confirms the adherence of the participating states to these principles and strengthens them to that extent.[94]

Thus the Final Act expanded the concept of what could be explored or, put another way, it eroded the size of that which fell within the exclusive domestic jurisdiction of a signatory state by allowing signatory states peaceful reaction to violations of human rights provisions.

The focus of this study now shifts to U.S. foreign policy in relation to the human rights provisions; consequently, the major issue is: What were the goals of U.S. foreign policy in the CSCE? Related to that question are two others: what were the likely consequences of U.S. policy at CSCE perceived to be and how was the national interest to be served by U.S. policy at the CSCE? It is to these questions that the chapter now turns.

U.S. National Interest and the CSCE

In writing about the U.S. national interest and the CSCE, three notes of caution should be kept in mind. First, this is being written in 1998, and the radical changes that occurred in international relations with the end of the Cold War and the demise of the Soviet Union make it difficult to evaluate policy on its own terms, in its own time, that is, from 1973 to 1980. Second, and related to the first, it is necessary to keep in mind there are limits to what foreign policy can accomplish even though radical change may suggest otherwise. Third, the term national interest is far from self-explanatory and thus needs to be characterized in context and clarified with reference to who is defining that interest.

During the Nixon-Kissinger era two major goals of foreign policy in relation to the Soviet Union were the maintenance of stability and the prevention of the expansion of Soviet influence in the international arena.

Détente, the term for the policy designed to accomplish these goals, included the development of a triangular relationship with China and the Soviet Union whereby the United States would play a balancing role between the other two states. Détente was to maintain peace and security, not by offering some panacea or utopian vision, but by establishing a pattern of relationships that would make the world safer and more stable. From Kissinger's perspective there really was no alternative to détente because anything else, including a foreign policy built on a human rights crusade, could only exacerbate tensions between the superpowers and thus increase the likelihood of nuclear war. By encouraging linkage across a wide range of issues, it was hoped the Soviet Union could be restrained from acting in a destabilizing manner. In addition, for Kissinger détente was a means of continuing the policy of containment. "Détente did not prevent resistance to Soviet expansion; on the contrary, it fostered the only possible psychological framework for such resistance."[95]

Both Nixon and Kissinger saw that the ideological struggle between the United States and Soviet Union would continue. Certainly neither man wanted to be perceived as being "soft on communism." Yet as Kissinger wrote:

> We did not consider a relaxation of tensions a concession to the Soviets. We had our own reasons for it. We were not abandoning the ideological struggle, but simply trying . . . to discipline it by precepts of national interest.[96]

Thus the concept of national interest, identified here with the maintenance of peace, was meant to restrain the ideological fervor that might provoke the unleashing of the Soviet Union's nuclear forces. Prudence and restraint would be the hallmarks of a policy seeking to avoid nuclear war. In a speech he gave in 1973, Kissinger asked, "How hard can we press without provoking the Soviet leadership into returning to practices in its foreign policy that increase international tensions?"[97] (As we have seen, in effect, even the Carter administration had to deal with this question, and it did so by lowering its human rights rhetoric.) In the same speech Kissinger explained:

Foreign policy must begin with the understanding that it involves relationships between sovereign countries. Sovereignty has been defined as a will uncontrolled by others; that is what gives foreign policy its contingent and ever incomplete character. . . . A nation's values define what is possible; its domestic structure decides what policies can in fact be implemented and sustained.[98]

It is unclear to what extent the definition of sovereignty given in this statement reflects actual practice today, but Kissinger's view about the contingent character and its origin in national sovereignty seems generally correct.

In the struggle with communism Kissinger saw a "long period of peace" favoring the pluralism of a democratic system over the Soviet system. In a memo to President Nixon (which the president underlined) Kissinger wrote:

The major, <u>long term question is whether the Soviets can hold their own bloc together while waiting for the West to succumb to a long period of relaxation</u> and to the temptations of economic competition. Certainly, our chances are as good as Brezhnev's, given the history of dissent in East Europe.[99]

This optimism and the modest goals of foreign policy that Kissinger pursued—increased safety and stability—were not enough to maintain public support for a foreign policy that, in the context of the Vietnam defeat and the Watergate scandal, seemed amoral if not immoral. Or as John Stoessinger put it, the modest goal which Kissinger sought was "a goal not quite in the mainstream of American history."[100]

For Presidents Nixon and Ford and for Secretary of State Kissinger, CSCE was a manifestation of the policy of détente. Especially early in the development of CSCE and the Final Act, the low profile the United States took represented the desire for a safer and more stable world order. It was believed that the consequences of the policy of détente would serve both the near-term and long-term interest of the United States. Thus the policy of détente is juxtaposed against the promotion of human rights.

In spite of the fact that Kissinger recognized, in his *Pacem in Terris* speech cited above, that the domestic structure "decides what policies can in fact be implemented and sustained,"[101] either because of flaws of articulation or conceptualization, American public opinion would not sustain détente. As Jeane Kirkpatrick noted:

> In retrospect it seems nearly inevitable that human rights should have become a central issue in American Foreign Policy once the U.S. became really involved in the world. The rights of individuals, whose protection we have always viewed as the purpose of a government, has always been a central preoccupation of America in politics. . . . Our identity is inextricably involved with the Declaration of Independence and Constitution. The notion that policy should not reflect concern with human rights and democracy is as farfetched as the notion that foreign policy should not express the nation.[102]

Of course it was up to Jimmy Carter to capitalize on that inevitability of emphasis on human rights. As both a candidate and a president he sensed the truth of Jeane Kirkpatrick's subsequent reflection:

> The notion that foreign policy should be guided by balance of power politics, or realpolitik, is utterly foreign to the American tradition and foreign to the American scene today. All our wars, beginning with the Revolutionary War, were justified in terms of the protection, the extension of universal human rights.[103]

It is important to note Kirkpatrick's use of the word "justified," because public justification may be quite different from the political leadership's real motivation. In subsequent chapters we shall explore this distinction more fully.

Dr. Kissinger, as a political realist, knew that for détente to be effective, he and the president needed the support of the American people. Yet he could not capture the moral imagination of the people to gain that support over the course of his tenure as secretary of state. President Carter, on the other hand, initially drew on that moral rhetoric, the rhetoric of a human rights crusade, to pursue his policy. In coming to office President Carter was not saying that he was against better relations with the Soviet Union (in short, he was not saying he was against détente), but he believed the goals of peace and human rights could be pursued simultaneously. He did not think détente and human rights were mutually exclusive. His goals were not dissimilar to Kissinger's, and President Carter ultimately gave a higher priority to détente than his initial rhetoric would have led one to believe. President Carter was effective in promoting human rights, even if not to the extent he would have liked. As John Stoessinger writes, "Jimmy Carter's personal influence was largely that of a catalyst. . . . In collisions with realpolitik, human rights were almost always sacrificed." [104] President Carter knew that, morally, one should not encourage nuclear war even if that meant being less outspoken on human rights. Even so the U.S. position on human rights in the context of CSCE was indeed vigorous.

The historical backgrounding provided by this chapter is meant to provide the data with which an ethic that is more concerned with the consequences of action than with maintenance of moral norms, as Christian realism is, must deal. One of the strengths of Christian realism is its willingness to address the concerns a responsible policymaker must face. Among the concepts a policymaker, and a Christian realist, uses is the idea of the national interest. The national interest, understood in terms of the capability to accomplish the goals of foreign policy, would have suffered if it had been expected to adopt a policy totally insensitive to human rights. On the other hand, a morality blinded to the danger that might accompany a human rights crusade would have been inadequate. A realistic foreign policy would take both détente and human rights into account as would a realistic morality.

Having addressed the contextual factors in the U.S.-Soviet relationship and their impact on the CSCE, the study will now turn to a description of Christian realism and a comparison of Christian realism with realism and idealism.

Notes

1. William Korey, *The Promises We Keep: Human Rights, the Helsinki Process, and American Foreign Policy*, with a foreword by Daniel Patrick Moynihan (N.Y.: St. Martin's Press, 1993), xvii-xix.

2. William Korey, *The Promises We Keep*, 61.

3. William Korey, *The Promises We Keep*, xviii.

4. John G. Stoessinger, *Nations in Darkness: China, Russia, and America*, 5th ed. (N.Y.: McGraw-Hill Publishing Company, 1990), 207.

5. John G. Stoessinger, *Nations in Darkness*, 208.

6. Adam B. Ulam, *Dangerous Relations: The Soviet Union in World Politics, 1970-1982* (N.Y.: Oxford University Press, 1983), 40.

7. Robert Dallek, *The American Style of Foreign Policy: Cultural Politics and Foreign Affairs* (N.Y.: Oxford University Press, 1983), 259, 261-62.

8. Ulam, *Dangerous Relations*, 46.

9. Henry A. Kissinger, *The White House Years* (Boston: Little, Brown and Company, 1979), 1136.

10. John J. Maresca, *To Helsinki: The Conference on Security and Cooperation in Europe 1973-1975*, new ed., with a foreword by William E. Griffith (Durham, N.C.: Duke University Press, 1987), 9.

11. Dallek, *The American Style of Foreign Policy*, 267.

12. Kissinger, *White House Years*, 54-55.

13. Stoessinger, *Nations in Darkness*, 216.

14. Kissinger, *White House Years*, 238-39.

15. Ulam, *Dangerous Relations*, 42.

16. Ulam, *Dangerous Relations*, 63.

17. Korey, *The Promises We Keep*, 5.

18. Gordon A. Craig and Alexander L. George, *Force and Statecraft: Diplomatic Problems of Our Time*, 2d ed. (N.Y.: Oxford University Press, 1990), 175.

19. Korey, *The Promises We Keep*, xxii.

20. Korey, *The Promises We Keep*, 1.

21. Craig and George, *Force and Statecraft*, 175.

22. Korey, *The Promises We Keep*, xxii.

23. Korey, *The Promises We Keep*, 2.

24. Henry Kissinger, *Years of Upheaval* (Boston: Little, Brown and Company, 1982), 986.

25. Joshua Muravchik, *The Uncertain Crusade: Jimmy Carter and the Dilemmas of Human Rights Policy*, with a foreword by Jeane Kirkpatrick (N.Y.: Hamilton Press, 1981), 17.

26. Muravchik, *The Uncertain Crusade*, 17, 23.

27. Muravchik, *The Uncertain Crusade*, 34.

28. Kissinger, *Years of Upheaval*, 240.

29. Kissinger, *Years of Upheaval*, 242.

30. Congress, House, Committee on Foreign Affairs, Subcommittee on International Organization and Movements, *Human Rights in the World Community: A Call for U.S. Leadership*, 93rd Cong., 2d sess., 27 March 1974, 3, 911.

31. House, *Human Rights in the World Community*, 11.

32. Congress, House, Committee on International Relations, Subcommittee on International Organizations, *Human Rights and United States Foreign Policy: A Review of the Administration's Record*, 95th Cong., 1st sess., 25 October 1977, 55.

33. Dante B. Fascell, "Did Human Rights Survive Belgrade?," *Foreign Policy* 31 (Summer 1978): 107.

34. Fascell, "Did Human Rights Survive Belgrade?"

35. Fascell, "Did Human Rights Survive Belgrade?," 107-8.

36. Margaret E. Galey, "Congress, Foreign Policy and Human Rights Ten Years After Helsinki" *Human Rights Quarterly: A Comparative and International Journal of the Social Sciences, Humanities and Law* 7 (August 1985): 337-38.

37. Ludmilla Alexeyeva, *Soviet Dissent: Contemporary Movements for National, Religious, and Human Rights*, trans. Carol Pearce and John Glad (Middletown, Conn.: Wesleyan University Press, 1985), 344.

38. Fascell, "Did Human Rights Survive Belgrade?," 110-11.

39. Fascell, "Did Human Rights Survive Belgrade?," 111.

40. Alexeyeva, *Soviet Dissent*, 335-36.

41. Alexeyeva, *Soviet Dissent*, 336.

42. Alexeyeva, *Soviet Dissent*

43. Alexeyeva, *Soviet Dissent*, 336, 338-39.

44. Alexeyeva, *Soviet Dissent*, 339.

45. Alexeyeva, *Soviet Dissent*, 341. See also Natan Sharansky, *Fear No Evil*, trans. Stefani Hoffman (N.Y.: Random House, 1988), xxi-xxii.

46. Alexeyeva, *Soviet Dissent*, 337.

47. Congress, House, Committee on International Relations, *Conference on Security and Cooperation in Europe: Hearing Before the Subcommittee on International Political and Military Affairs of the Committee on International Relations*, 94th Cong., 1st sess., 6 May 1975, 2.

48. House, *Conference on Security and Cooperation in Europe*, 23.

49. Maresca, *To Helsinki*, 10-11.

50. Maresca, *To Helsinki*, 4.

51. Maresca, *To Helsinki*, 11.

52. Maresca, *To Helsinki*.

53. Maresca, *To Helsinki.*, 46.

54. Maresca, *To Helsinki.*, xii.

55. Maresca, *To Helsinki.*, xii.

56. Korey, *The Promises We Keep*, xix-xx.

57. Korey, *The Promises We Keep*, xxiv-xxv.

58. Gaddis Smith, *Morality, Reason, and Power: American Diplomacy in the Carter Years* (N.Y.: Hill and Wang, 1986), 31.

59. John G. Stoessinger, *Crusaders and Pragmatists: Movers of Modern American Foreign Policy*, 2d ed. (N.Y.: W.W. Norton and Company, 1985), 252-53. Christian realism, as Niebuhr states it, would assert that it may be something of an overstatement to say that the United States is different from other countries in requiring a moral justification for foreign policy, but the basic thought, which the criticism of Kissinger focused on the need for a moral rationale, seems correct.

60. Stoessinger, *Crusaders and Pragmatists*, 67-68.

61. Muravchik, *The Uncertain Crusade*, 31.

62. Muravchik, *The Uncertain Crusade,* 31.

63. Muravchik, *The Uncertain Crusade*, 34.

64. Quoted in Smith, *Morality, Reason, and Power*, 52-53.

65. Smith, *Morality, Reason, and Power*, 52-53.

66. Fascell, "Did Human Rights Survive Belgrade?," 109.

67. Korey, *The Promises We Keep*, 82.

68. Korey, *The Promises We Keep*, 82.

69. Korey, *The Promises We Keep*, 84.

70. Max M. Kampelman, *Entering New Worlds: The Memoirs of a Private Man in Public Life* (N.Y.: Harper Collins, 1991), 221-22.

71. Fascell, "Did Human Rights Survive Belgrade?," 112.

72. Fascell, "Did Human Rights Survive Belgrade?," 116.

73. Alexeyeva, *Soviet Dissent*, 344-45.

74. Alexeyeva, *Soviet Dissent*, 346-47.

75. Fascell, "Did Human Rights Survive Belgrade?," 104-5.

76. Fascell, "Did Human Rights Survive Belgrade?," 115.

77. Korey, *The Promises We Keep*, xxvi.

78. Korey, *The Promises We Keep*, xxvi.

79. Korey, *The Promises We Keep*, xxvii.

80. For an analysis of all three experiences see Smith, *Morality, Reason, and Power*, 191-93, 197, 2162-4.

81. Suzanne Bastid, "The Special Significance of the Helsinki Final Act," in *Human Rights, International Law and the Helsinki Accord,* ed. Thomas Buergenthal assisted by Judith R. Hall, published under the auspices of the American Society of International Law, LandMark Studies (N.Y.: Allanheld, Osman Universe Books, 1977), 12.

82. Igor I. Kavass, Jacqueline Poquin Granier and Mary Francis Dominick, eds., *Human Rights, European Politics, and the Helsinki Accord:*

The Documentary Evolution of the Conference on Security and Cooperation in Europe 19731975 (Buffalo, N.Y.: William S. Hein and Co., Inc., 1981), ix-xiii.

83. State Department, *Bulletin Reprint*, "Final Act, Helsinki, 1975," 16.

84. State Department, *Bulletin Reprint*, 615.

85. State Department, *Bulletin Reprint*, 16.

86. State Department, *Bulletin Reprint*, 17.

87. State Department, *Bulletin Reprint*, 19.

88. Ulam, *Dangerous Relations: The Soviet Union in World Politics 19701982*, 142-43.

89. Virginia Leary, "The Implementation of the Human Rights Provisions of the Helsinki Final Act A Preliminary Assessment: 1975-1977," in *Human Rights, International Law and the Helsinki Accord*, ed. Thomas Buergenthal, 156.

90. Muravchik, *The Uncertain Crusade*, 83-84.

91. Bastid, "The Significance of the Helsinki Final Act," 13.

92. Bastid, "The Significance of the Helsinki Final Act," 14.

93. Thomas Buergenthal, "International Human Rights Law in the Helsinki Final Act: Conclusions," in *Human Rights, International Law and the Helsinki Accord*, ed. Thomas Buergenthal, 6.

94. Buergenthal, *Human Rights, International Law and the Helsinki Accord*.

95. Kissinger, *Years of Upheaval*, 237.

96. Kissinger, *Years of Upheaval.*, 236-37.

97. Quoted in Maresca, *To Helsinki*, 35.

98. Maresca, *To Helsinki*, 35.

99. Kissinger, *Years of Upheaval*, 243.

100. Stoessinger, *Crusaders and Pragmatists*, 208.

101. Maresca, *To Helsinki*, 35.

102. Jeane Kirkpatrick, foreword to Muravchik, *The Uncertain Crusade*, ix.

103. Kirkpatrick, *Uncertain Crusade*, xi.

104. Stoessinger, *Crusaders and Pragmatists*, 283.

Chapter 2

Morality and U.S. Foreign Policy

The previous chapter examined the development of U.S. policy in relation to the Helsinki Accord. This chapter moves on to define Christian realism and its part in the debate over the proper role of morality in the formulation and execution of foreign policy. The role of morality in international relations is a question that raises fundamental concerns about the nature of the international system as well as about the nature of human nature. Questions that this chapter will address are: What is the nature of the positions of the moralistic or legalistic school of international relations and the realist school? How does the Christian realist approach differ from that of the conventional moralist and conventional realist and what are the unique benefits of Christian realism? What role, if any, should Christian ethics play in the development of foreign policy?

In dealing with the issue of morality in foreign policy the chapter will attempt to avoid two pitfalls, confusing morality as the content of policy with moralistic rhetoric promoting policy and succumbing to the temptation to see no concern at all for morality in realism. In regard to the first pitfall one should note that promoting human rights (a moral value) may be accomplished through quiet diplomacy, for example. Thus, while quiet diplomacy may not satisfy those requiring moralistic rhetoric, it may qualify as a moral element in foreign policy. In regard to the temptation to see no concern at all for morality in political realism, it will be shown that even the political scientist most known for his support of realism, Hans Morgenthau, saw a limited role for morality in foreign policy.

It may be hoped that common ground may be found between the two groups of theorists. If the international system is not anarchic, if there is a society at the international level, if policymakers justify policies in the language of internationally shared values, then there may exist enough common ground between realists and liberal internationalists to talk of morality in foreign policy. This is not to suggest that there are no differences between the two groups. This is merely to suggest that for realists there are value considerations in foreign policy, and for the idealists the values can take into account human limitations and with moral maturity accept that there is no ultimate fulfillment of history in history.

The chapter will begin with a description of the problem of either raising or not raising moral norms in making foreign policy. It will then describe the moralistic and realistic approaches to foreign policy, and then describe Christian realism in contrast to these two. In order to illustrate the strengths of the Christian realist approach, the characterization of that approach by Charles Frankel will be critiqued. By way of summary a section devoted to morality and foreign policy will conclude the chapter and relate the material to church involvement on the Helsinki Final Act.

The Problem

In determining the proper role, if any, for morality in international relations one should distinguish the differences among moralistic rhetoric, moral norms, and morality. Political realism emphasizes the incorrectness of moralistic rhetoric without necessarily rejecting all ethical considerations in political policy.[1] Thus moralistic rhetoric may decry policy for being immoral, whereas the policy may merely be couched in terms not associated with moral norms. It is theoretically possible for moral norms to be at the heart of policy without that policy being promoted in moralistic rhetoric. (It should be noted that one of the roles of moralistic rhetoric is to gain public support for a policy. It is therefore difficult to imagine a policy concerned with ethics not employing such rhetoric.)

Political scientist Joseph S. Nye Jr. points out that those who make ethical judgments tend to weigh three dimensions—motives, means, and consequences.[2] Unfortunately for those who make foreign policy, the ambiguity inherent in policymaking extends to all three dimensions. Yet even if it is clear that the policymaker has the best intentions and means, the consequences are not necessarily predictable and thus capable of being used to evaluate whether a particular policy is moral or not.

In addition to the ambiguity inherent in setting foreign policy, there is a structural obstacle to moral choice in international relations. The international arena is akin to "a state of nature," as that term is often used by political theorists. (The concept of a state of nature is a theoretical construct of what life is like prior to the institution of society and government.) The state of nature could vary greatly in the amount of violence people engage in, but it tends to be more chaotic and anarchical than society as we who are under government know it. Seen from the perspective of this anarchial condition, there is a significant difference between action in the international sphere and in the domestic area. There is a difference between individual and group action in domestic order and the statesman's action on the world scene.

> In the first place, in a domestic system which functions well, individuals and groups can behave morally because there is a frame work of social order—in which they have a stake. *A contrario*, when that framework disappears, and survival or basic needs become the obsession of all, individuals and groups start behaving in an immoral or in a cowardly way. . . . The second stage of the argument shows that this contrast between the behavior of individuals and groups in the domestic order and the statesman is particularly acute. . . . The statesman operating in the context of domestic politics can often behave reasonably well . . . especially when the political system and the social order are recognized as legitimate, and of course also because of the state's monopoly on coercion. But a statesman in the international competition cannot afford moral behavior so easily; first, because of what might be called the state's duty of selfishness. . . . Secondly, in international relations, by contrast with domestic politics, the scope of moral conflict is infinite, whereas in domestic order the scope is

normally much more restricted. Thirdly, violence, the ever-present possibility of war, limits the range of moral opportunity. There is the state's security dilemma, there is the need to survive. And because a drastic separation between order and justice exists in international affairs, the state has to survive first; as a statesman, you have to establish or preserve order first, and then you can worry about justice, if there is time left. International order has to be established or defended every minute, whereas domestic order is a given and already reflects a conception of justice.[3]

Given this quasianarchy, where security can be provided only by each individual nation itself, since there is no overarching authority, it should not be surprising that the fundamental moral axiom is self-preservation. It should be noted that the lack of community at the international level gives rise to world government schemes that take into account the significant differences between domestic and international politics without giving adequate attention to the reasons for anarchy at the international level.

In terms of the structure not of the international arena but of international relations, one should keep in mind that the realist argument deals with politics at its foundation. The struggle for power that is at the heart of pursuing the national interest deals with the basic instrument of political power—the use of force. The moralist or legalist argument, on the other hand, often makes its most efficacious arguments not in relation to high politics but in the more mundane, but just as frequent, interactions on trade, commerce, and international exchanges. This suggests that neither approach may deal comprehensively with all aspects of international relations. Reinhold Niebuhr makes the point that for the statesman there is an additional obstacle to moral action as generally conceived in Christian ethics. The ethical ideal in the Christian faith is *agape*, sacrificial love, symbolized in the crucifixion of Jesus of Nazareth. Yet the statesman, who in his personal life ought to attempt to live out the sacrificial love, would be acting irresponsibly and immorally if he sacrificed his nation. The policymaker has a responsibility to others that prevents him or her from sacrificing them.[4]

Current examples abound of the difficulty in relating morality to foreign policy. The United States has given most favored nation (MFN) trading status to the Peoples' Republic of China after its clear violations of human rights both before and after the suppression of the 1989 Tiananmen Square pro-democracy movement. Does this seem like a moral policy? Is the United States not rewarding policies it theoretically abhors? Would not a moral U.S. foreign policy withhold MFN status until China liberalized its human rights policies? When the United States goes ahead with MFN status with China, it seems somehow to give credence to the argument that either human rights issues are matters of a nation's internal affairs (and thus not subject to international sanction) or human rights are a Western concept and not in fact universally applicable. On the other hand, if MFN status were not given, would not the United States lose leverage with China and thereby actually be in a poorer position to encourage improvement in China's human rights practices? If MFN status were withheld would not the strained relations actually cost American jobs and thereby weaken the United States? These questions are raised not to support one approach or the other but to indicate the complexity of relating morality to setting foreign policy.

Another contemporary example of the difficulty of relating morality to foreign policy is the question: What should U.S. policy be in Bosnia? Is it moral to ignore the "ethnic cleansing" being carried out by the Serbs on the Muslim population? Would it be more moral to intervene militarily without clear objectives or a clear declaration of support from the American people? Would it be a moral policy to intervene militarily on behalf of the Bosnian Muslims if that led to a wider war? Once again these questions are meant to suggest the moral ambiguity surrounding foreign policy.

A final contemporary example illustrating not only the difficulty of relating morality to foreign policy but also the anarchical nature of international society is that of the U.S. policy toward Haiti, in restoring democracy to that country. Certainly the Clinton administration's policy of restoring Jean Bertrand Aristide to the presidency of Haiti as a means of restoring democracy was morally worthwhile. The mission of Jimmy Carter that allowed the U.S. goal to be accomplished with a minimum of violence seems laudable. But would not a better policy, in a better world, have been to have the United States (or the UN itself), representing the community of nations, punish those responsible for ending democracy in Haiti? Would not an approach that punished dictators give more legitimacy to international law and organization and add stability to already existing democracies? Once again these questions are raised to illustrate how morality relates to foreign policy, and, in this example at least, how a vision of world order may inform the debate.

Historical ambiguity, international anarchy, and the limitations upon the policymaker as representative of a nation interact in such a way as to severely limit the operation of moral norms in setting foreign policy. There are those moralists and legalists who argue the primacy of moral norms in overcoming the ambiguity, anarchy, and limitations on decision-makers. The realists counter that the ambiguity, anarchy, and limitations are the "givens" of policymaking in foreign affairs and that any morality concerned with the consequences of policy must take those givens into account to be morally responsible. It is to an examination of those respective positions that we now turn.

The Moralistic or Legalistic Approach

In attempting to understand the moralistic or legalistic approach to international relations it might help to identify a few examples of those who were promoting such an approach in America during this century. The years between World War I and World War II saw a large number of persons, sometimes referred to as internationalists, making the claim for the role of moral norms in international relations. Alfred Zimmern, professor of international relations at Oxford University; Gilbert Murray, president of the League of Nations Union; Nicholas Murray Butler, president of Columbia University; and James T. Shotwell, architect of the Kellogg-Briand Pact, were among the most prominent members of this school of thought.[5] These people, who believed in the notion of human progress, saw three means by which morality could influence foreign policy. The first was the use of domestic public opinion to forge a moral foreign policy. The second method for infusing morality into international relations was the use of the court of world public opinion represented by the League of Nations. The final route by which morality could influence foreign policy was through its effect on the consciences of individual national leaders.[6] The proponents of this school of thought made four claims about the role of morality in foreign policy.

They claimed that relatively clear international moral norms existed that could guide state decision makers in pursuing just policies. They argued that domestic public opinion could serve as an effective moral constraint upon the actions of state decision makers. The internationalists advanced a view of human nature that stressed rationality and community, rather than conflict and the drive for power. And they believed that World War I and the democratization of the West had created a radically new situation for international relations in which morally based precepts of state action could be effectively enforced by international public opinion and the community of nations.[7]

Each of these points will be challenged, as we shall see, by the realists writing later. The context in which these people articulated their moralistic and legalistic approach to international affairs should be remembered. President Woodrow Wilson represented the kind of statesman who, moralists thought, epitomized the ethical leader. In the inter-war years there was a tremendous emphasis on the role of international law and, in particular, mediation of disputes. The founding of the League of Nations, even though the United States was not a member, represented greater reliance on law and less on power politics. In short, the post-World War I political environment nurtured into the optimism expressed by the moralistic-legalistic school. The reverse may be said as well; that the ineffectiveness of the League in dealing with the crisis in Ethiopia, the crisis in Manchuria, and the rearmament of Germany led to disillusionment, which in turn led to the search for a more adequate explanation of international relations. It should be noted that the League mandate system, by which the Allies divided up the colonial territories of the defeated powers, seemed to provide a hypocritical mask for traditional imperialism, despite the mandate system's intention to encourage ultimate mandate independence.[8]

Yet it would be a mistake to make both schools a reaction to events in the twentieth century, for both have deep historical roots. The realist school looks as far back as Thucydides, in the fifth century B.C., to his history of the Peloponnesian War for a description of how international relations operates. For the moralists, the writings of Immanuel Kant, in the eighteenth century, were particularly important in articulating a solution to the problem of war.

Kant, in his essay translated either as "Perpetual Peace" or "Eternal Peace," outlines the requirements for a world order which would assure peace. In the essay he frequently refers to international law, but it is clear that the term "law" has a moral quality, as when he writes:

> This homage which every state renders the concept of law (at least in words) seems to prove that there exists in man a greater moral quality (although at present a dormant one), to try and master the evil element in him (which he cannot deny), and to hope for this in others.[9]

Morality relates to international relations in another way as well. According to Kant, a good political constitution is not the result of advanced morality but rather a good moral condition results from a good constitution.[10] He points out that in a "natural state" there is not a state of peace but a state of war. To overcome that natural state of war a legal constitution must be adopted of which there are three kinds. The first type of constitution is formed according to the right of individual citizenship in a nation (*jus civitatis*). The second constitution is one whose principle is international law, which determines the relations of states (*jus gentium*). The third constitution is formed in accordance with cosmopolitan law, insofar as individuals may be thought of as citizens of one worldstate (*jus cosmopoliticum*).[11] The prescription Kant presents is one of a pact among liberal republican governments that would encourage proper behavior among states and thus limit war. In addition, his cosmopolitan law reflecting a world society would undergird such a rule of law. He saw the development of commerce assisting in the development of a peaceful order, even if not for reasons of morality.[12] The purpose of this brief description of Kant's thought on peace is to indicate the historic character of the moralistic-legalistic perspective. It is also to indicate, in light of what will be said about international law, the stability of the concept of law as an expression of morality in international relations. Because of the continuing attractiveness of his approach to peace, Kant receives attention among political philosophers. While it would be easy to exaggerate, one distinction between the perspectives of the moralist school and the realist school is that the former is more concerned with prescription and the latter with description. Thus far, this essay has addressed primarily the question of how morality, for the moralists or legalists, should impact international relations. Let us turn now to the nature of the international system as seen by the moralist.

The League of Nations, and by extension the United Nations, was designed as a means to replace the balance of power system, extolled by the realists, with a collective security system. The criticism of Europe's balance of power was that it simply did not work to restrain violence. The balance of power system, based on the recognition of a nation's own interest and ability to shift alliances to prevent any one nation or alliance from gaining too much power and thereby being tempted to adventurist military action, was to be replaced. The collective security system would eschew alliances for a system whereby overwhelming force could be brought to bear against a nation that broke international law. In the collective security arrangement the law would be clear and the force aligned against a lawbreaker would be quick and sufficiently powerful to punish the lawbreaker. Any potential aggressor (aggression being perceived as the most egregious form of lawbreaking) would be deterred from disrupting the peace as defined by the League.

President Wilson was critical of the balance of power system. He saw it as both ineffective and immoral. Clearly, for a president engaged in fighting a war that was seen as a result of the balance of power system, it would have been hard to come to any other conclusion than that the system was ineffective in preventing war. In addition, President Wilson thought the system was immoral.

> It stood . . . for selfish rivalry among autocratic cliques; secret and devious maneuvering; ruthless intrigue; cynical bargaining and unconscionable bartering of helpless and innocent people; sacrificing the interests of peoples to the ambitions of militaristic tyrants.[13]

President Wilson argued that the anti-German forces had fought:

> to do away with an old order and to establish a new one, and the center and characteristic of the old order was that unstable thing which we used to call the "balance of power"—a thing in which the balance was determined by the sword which was thrown in [on] the one side or the

other; a balance which was determined by the unstable equilibrium of
competitive interests; a balance which was maintained by jealous
watchfulness and an antagonism of interests which, though it was
generally latent, was always deep-seated.[14]

Thus one finds President Wilson, as a representative of the moralistic or
legalistic perspective, rejecting the system that characterized European
international politics in the nineteenth century.

If one examines both the League of Nations and the United Nations as
expressions of Wilsonian criticism of the balance of power, it is
nonetheless clear that power was not neglected. In particular, the
organizing principles of the United Nations take into account the realities
of power and the need for stability. Two underlying assumptions were to
operate in the United Nations. First, there was to be a Great Power
accord; otherwise the veto would be employed in the Security Council,
and the UN would be unable to field a military force. Second, instead of
balancing alliance against alliance, the theory of collective security
postulates an alliance of power against a lawbreaker. With the assumption
of major power collaboration, guaranteed by the veto, the power
configuration is taken into account but not seen as a serious obstacle to
substituting collective security for the balance of power system. In short it
is almost assumed that a sufficient sense of justice exists in the
international arena to supplant the balancing of alliances and interests.

It should not be surprising to find Americans attracted to replacing a
balance of power system with a system promising order on the basis of the
rule of law. A domestic analogy arises for Americans who see law as
reflecting morality; therefore, international law would reflect morality. (It
should be kept in mind that human rights embodied in international law
are often perceived by Americans to be a validation of American morality.
This is so, even though international human rights agreements often
highlight economic and social rights that Americans have not always
championed.) Power is less clearly at stake in a world where all one need
do is identify a lawbreaker and punish the wayward nation. The
assumption seems to be that for peace to exist, it is less necessary to
discover what interests nations share (and how those interests are to be
shared) than it is for the community of nations simply to articulate the
values upon which justice rests.

In two other ways this liberal internationalist approach appears attractive to Americans. First, it rests on a clear domestic analogy. Within the United States people and organizations are protected by an overarching structure of law. Second, and related to the first, the liberal internationalist approach relies on the development of a world constitution or covenant. Americans tend to think the United States was a creation of the covenant known as the Constitution. Thus, American experience seems to confirm the ability of people to create out of chaos a document that will create community. This covenantal concern finds expression in proposals for a reformed United Nations capable of enforcing peace such as Grenville Clark and Louis B. Sohn's *World Peace through World Law* (1960) and Harold Stassen's *Draft Charter for a New United Nations* (1985).

The moralist (Kant), the politician (Wilson), and the legalist (Stassen) will all find themselves criticized for not taking seriously the organic features of civil community that are necessary preconditions for peace. If the balance of power can be criticized as a "system" for maintaining peace, it may nevertheless be a helpful concept in establishing other instruments for peace. Between excellent analysis of the anarchy that characterizes the international system and the prescription of world peace through world law lies a much needed understanding of the dynamics inherent in the behavior of nationstates. It is here that the realists level their most significant criticism of the moralists.

To summarize the position of the moralists, there are moral norms that are widely shared and universally applicable to the behavior of nations and people. These moral standards can and should form the basis for a world order. This universal morality is expressed in terms of international law. Since the norms need merely find expression to gain assent by the people of the world and their republican governments, the major task is to construct the right legal constitution. The aim of foreign policy should be to attain such a constitution. With such a legal framework in place, a nation's primary interest, security, would be guaranteed by the community; the struggle over articulating and promoting the national interest would be minimized and war would be less likely. The balance of power system would be replaced by a collective security system. It is to a critique of this position that we now turn.

The Realist Perspective

The realist position is most frequently identified with the political scientist
Hans Morgenthau, the Christian ethicist Reinhold Niebuhr, and, for the
purposes of this study, the historian and diplomat Henry Kissinger.
Because of Niebuhr's unique contribution in explicitly bringing
transcendent norms to bear on the concept of national interest, this section
will discuss his views last.

As the most academically influential American scholar of political
realism, Hans Morgenthau's writings will form the basis for the
discussion of non-Christian political realism.[15] For Hans Morgenthau the
relationship between morality and foreign policy may be summed up in the
statement:

> Neither science nor ethics nor politics can resolve the conflict between
> politics and ethics into harmony. We have no choice between power
> and the common good. To act successfully, that is, according to the
> rules of the political art, is political wisdom. To know with despair that
> the political act is inevitably evil, and to act nevertheless, is moral
> courage. To choose among several expedient actions the least evil one
> is moral judgment. In the combination of political wisdom, moral
> courage, and moral judgment, man reconciles his political nature with
> his moral destiny. That this conciliation is nothing more than a *modus
> vivendi*, uneasy, precarious, and even paradoxical, can disappoint only
> those who prefer to gloss over and to distort the tragic contradictions of
> human existence with the soothing logic of a specious concord.[16]

One sees here that Morgenthau is concerned to evaluate policy on the
basis of its consequences couched in the language of moral norms as he
understood them. The ability to act according to the rules of political art
means the ability to maintain or extend one's power or the power of one's
nation. There is in his thinking no overarching moral principle, at least as
moralists generally conceive of such principles, controlling the process.
Expediency in selecting the least evil action as a characteristic of moral
judgment seldom recommends itself to the moralist. Morgenthau's
awareness of the "tragic contradictions of human existence" is repeated
too in the thought of Kissinger and Niebuhr. All of this suggests an

awareness of human sinfulness and the complexity of personal as well as international interaction.

In *Politics among Nations* Morgenthau identifies six principles of political realism. The first principle is that political realism believes that politics is governed by objective laws rooted in human nature. The second principle asserts that the "main signpost that helps political realism to find its way through the landscape of international politics is the concept of interest defined in terms of power."[17] The third principle makes clear that the concept of interest defined as power is an objective category that is universally valid, but interest does not have a fixed static meaning. Fourth, political realism is aware that political action has moral significance.[18] Fifth, political realism does not identify the moral aspirations of a particular nation with universal moral laws. The final principle is that the difference between political realism and other schools of thought is real.[19] The political realist sees power as the economist deals with wealth, and the moralist sees action in light of moral principles.

It should be noted in light of the fourth principle that the political realist is aware of both the demands of politics and that political actions have moral significance. Even though the realist is aware that there is moral significance to political action, for the realist this does not mean that the political requirements are subsumed by moral demands. A tension, as Morgenthau's statement suggests, is maintained between the two. In short, the fourth principle does not qualify the realist's commitment to the national interest, politically understood.

These principles are intended to add rationality to understanding international relations in spite of the fact that from the standpoint of the international system any nation may behave irrationally. Operating in the national interest is in keeping with realist theory, even though it may not seem in keeping with a moralist's conception of the good of the international community. The realist's argument is that nations do operate on the basis of their national interest as they perceive it. Nations seek to maintain or expand their power in order to enhance their security and their prestige.

For Morgenthau morality enters into international relations in three ways: as ideological justification for promotion of a nation's self-interested foreign policy, as an element that distorts formulation of policy, and as a means for promoting the moral worth of national interest.[20] It is clear from his writings that Morgenthau is most concerned with preventing the moralist from distorting foreign policy, and it is toward that end he writes:

> There can be no political morality without prudence; that is, without consideration of the political consequences of seemingly moral action. Realism . . . considers prudence—to be the supreme virtue in politics. Ethics in the abstract judges action by its conformity with the moral law; political ethics judges action by its political consequences.[21]

This prudence is and must be, according to Morgenthau, of utmost concern to the policymaker since the security and survival of the nation are at stake.

Morgenthau's criticism of the idealist or moralist emphasizes two major points. First, the world-embracing principles presented by the moralist are too vague and general to provide guidance for policy. Second, the idealist poses parochial interests in the dress of universal moral principles, which then presupposes those who do not agree with those principles to be less moral.[22]

In spite of the statements above there is in Morgenthau's approach a transcendent element. Morgenthau is concerned with morality as seen in his opposition to the Vietnam War. Morgenthau's position on the Vietnam War prompted Henry Kissinger to write:

> Even Hans Morgenthau, the doyen of American philosophers of the national interest, was moved to a proclamation of America's immorality: "When we talk about the violation of the rules of war, we must keep in mind that the fundamental violation, from which all other specific violations follow, is the very waging of this kind of war."[23]

Morgenthau does make a distinction between the United States and the Soviet Union. His concern that American preoccupation with morality in foreign policy is hypocritical really is a moral judgment, not a political one.[24] His emphasis on the national interest is for him a moral argument, in that national interest has moral dignity. This is so because the national community is the only source of order and the only protector of minimal moral values in a world that lacks order and moral consensus.[25]

It is at this point that the prescriptive differences between the realist and the idealist become most clear. To the realist, the "givenness" of the international system requires nations to act in their own self-interest, synonymous with moderate and restrained diplomacy. To the idealist, the "givenness" of the international system requires revelation of a universal moral consensus and community. Both the realist and the idealist are seeking an order that allows morality to develop. Nevertheless, there is an obvious tension here between the two perspectives as to which world vision is most likely to enhance the development of morality.

As noted above, a principle of political realism is that it does not identify the moral aspirations of a particular nation with moral laws of universal applicability. Yet if one carries relativism too far, how does one make a distinction between the policies of a Hitler and those of Wilson? It is possible that simply because a value, such as human rights, has its origin in a particular setting it does not mean it is not applicable in other societies.

The realist warns against a moralism that does not take into account sufficiently the proposition that nations usually act in their self-interest. According to the realist, in failing to consider self-interest the moralist's prescription tends to be illusory, ineffectual, deceptive, or fanatic.[26] The concept of national interest itself may seem to ignore morality without actually doing so. In the discussion that follows, one of the points to be made is that Niebuhr's Christian realism holds a view that characterizes national interest in such a way as to take into account the interests of other nations.

Morgenthau emphasizes the difference between principle and national interest because for him principle is too transcendent and human nature too flawed to inform the formulation of policy. Thus, he is ambivalent on the relation between transcendent norm and policy. It is at this point that the Christian realism of Reinhold Niebuhr differs from the realism of Morgenthau. Robert Good points to the difference when he writes:

> What Morgenthau and Kennan only imply, Niebuhr makes perfectly explicit. There can be no health in the society of men unless the claims of interest are challenged by a loyalty larger than interest, just as loyalty to principle must be chastened by a sober awareness of the force of interest. Niebuhr's straightforwardness is to be preferred. . . . The

justifiable responsibilities of the statesman to his constituency, combined with the power of "collective self-concern," place the virtue of self-giving beyond the moral possibilities of nations. Yet reference to such norms as justice and equality, order and mutuality, ought to provide both a directive for and a judgment upon policy as the statesman searches for a concurrence between the nation's interest and the general welfare.[27]

Niebuhr is adding a creative tension between transcendent norm and national interest. It is less that the realism of Niebuhr contradicts that of Morgenthau than that it supplements it.

Niebuhr begins his criticism of the moralist's approach by criticizing the practice of rooting political and legal theory in political institutions and processes rather than probing deeper to the level of human nature.[28] As Morgenthau did, Niebuhr emphasizes power. Niebuhr sees the human quest for power as a means to overcome anxiety. He points out that the will to live is spiritually transmuted into the will to power.

Man, being more than a natural creature, is not interested merely in physical survival but in prestige and social approval. Having the intelligence to anticipate the perils in which he stands in nature and history, he invariably seeks to gain security against these perils by enhancing his power, individually and collectively. Possessing a darkly unconscious sense of his insignificance in the total scheme of things, he seeks to compensate for his insignificance by pretensions of pride. The conflicts between men are thus never simple conflicts between competing survival impulses. They are conflicts in which each man or group seeks to guard its power and prestige against the peril of competing expressions of power and pride. Since the very possession of power and prestige always involves some encroachments upon the prestige and power of others, this conflict is by its very nature a more stubborn and difficult one than the mere competition between various survival impulses in nature. . . . [T]his conflict expresses itself even more cruelly in collective than in individual terms.[29]

Here Niebuhr is providing the foundation for the realist's emphasis on power as well as the basic reason why the idealist's perspective seems so inadequate in addressing the problem of war. This analysis is essential for seeing the self-interest in all human endeavor. Yet to know the power and pervasiveness of self-interest is not meant to give it moral justification.[30] For Niebuhr, adequate policy can come only from giving in to neither cynicism nor utopianism.

It might be stated, somewhat parenthetically, that the current evaluation of Niebuhr among nongovernmental activists as well as politicians and scholars rests on answering whether or not Niebuhr was able to walk the line between cynicism and utopianism. For activists in the "peace movement" Niebuhr is often characterized as a Cold Warrior whose evaluation of human nature and the evils of Soviet communism contributed more to confrontation with the possibility of nuclear war than to détente.

Let us evaluate more fully the thought of Niebuhr by seeing why liberal internationalists might criticize him. It has been noted that Niebuhr sought to expand the concept of national interest by acknowledging a capacity for justice to prevent interest from being seen too narrowly. "Politics will, to the end of history, be an area where conscience and power meet, where the ethical and coercive factors of human life will interpenetrate and work out their tentative and uneasy compromises."[31] According to Robert McElroy, the problem with Niebuhr's anthropology is that while he demonstrates how morality is circumscribed in international relations, "it is difficult to project how justice takes on a substantive role."[32] This type of response to Niebuhr's Christian realism seems to be interpreted by Niebuhr as saying, "We understand your realism but where is the hope of the Christian faith?"

The hope is difficult to discern from Niebuhr's writing because of three related emphases. First, he writes against a liberal moral perfectionism that he perceives as a Christian heresy. Second, he writes against a cultural faith in progress in history. Third, he writes against a faith in the ability of human rationality to create institutions that in turn create community.

While Niebuhr makes these points at many places in his writings, one of the clearest expressions of these emphases is in his introduction to his 1940 work, *Christianity and Power Politics*. In stating the thesis of the book he writes:

The thesis is that modern Christian and secular perfectionism, which places a premium upon nonparticipation in conflict, is a very sentimentalized version of the Christian faith and is at variance with the profoundest insights of the Christian religion. . . . The "liberal culture" of modern bourgeois civilization has simply and sentimentally transmuted the suprahistorical ideals of perfection of the gospel into simple historical possibilities. In consequence it defines the good man and the good nation as the man and nation which avoid conflict. Sometimes it merely insists that violent conflict must be avoided. But this finally comes to the same thing because the foe may always threaten us with violent reaction to our nonviolent forms of pressure, in which case we must desist from pressing our cause or cease to be "good." . . . It is the thesis of these essays that modern liberal perfectionism actually distills moral perversity out of its moral absolutes. It is unable to make significant distinctions between tyranny and freedom because it can find no democracy pure enough to deserve its devotion; and in any case it can find none which is not involved in conflict, in its effort to defend itself against tyranny. It is unable to distinguish between the peace of capitulation to tyranny and the peace of the Kingdom of God. It does not realize that its effort to make the peace of the Kingdom of God into a simple historical possibility must inevitably result in placing a premium upon surrender to evil, because the alternative course involves men and nations in conflict, or runs the risk, at least, of involving them in conflict.[33]

By making suprahistorical ideals of perfection realizable in history, the Christian really fails to appreciate both the depth of self-interestedness in human affairs and the ability for the self to transcend the self. The cultural perfectionist fails to see the profound evil at the center of all human action. In making the ideals of perfection realizable in history, Christian faith loses its prophetic role. That is, if perfect love is a possibility then it no longer stands in judgment of all human love and justice.

Even though Niebuhr criticizes pacifism, he allows for a type of pacifism that is in keeping with the Christian faith.

In one of its aspects modern Christian pacifism is simply a version of Christian perfectionism. It expresses a genuine impulse to take the law of Christ seriously and not to allow the political strategies, which the sinful character of man makes necessary, to become final norms. In its profounder forms this Christian perfectionism did not proceed from a simple faith that the "law of Love" could be regarded as an alternative to the political strategies by which the world achieves a precarious justice. These strategies invariably involve the balancing of power with power; and they never completely escape the peril of tyranny on the one hand, and the peril of anarchy and warfare on the other. In medieval ascetic perfectionism and in Protestant sectarian perfectionism (of the type of Menno Simons, for instance) the effort to achieve a standard of perfect love in individual life was not presented as a political alternative. On the contrary, the political problem and task were specifically disavowed. This perfectionism did not give itself to the illusion that it had discovered a method for eliminating the element of conflict from political strategies. On the contrary, it regarded the mystery of evil as beyond its power of solution. It was content to set up the most perfect and unselfish individual life as a symbol of the Kingdom of God. It knew that this could only be done by disavowing the political task and by freeing the individual of all responsibility for social justice.[34]

Thus Reinhold Niebuhr is not criticizing all pacifism, only that pacifism meant to guide policy. There is an appropriate role for Christian perfectionism and that is to uphold the ideal of love. Unfortunately, most modern forms of Christian pacifism are heretical in that they reflect the Renaissance faith in the goodness of humanity and reject the Christian doctrine of original sin.[35]

Along with his criticism of moral perfectionism Niebuhr takes exception to modern culture's faith in history.

Though all human capacities are subject to development and the cultural achievements and social institutions of mankind are capable of indeterminate development, the extension of human power and freedom in either individual life or in the total human enterprise does not change the human situation essentially. Man remains a creature of nature on every stage of his development. There are certain bounds of human finiteness which no historical development can overcome. The preoccupation of modern culture with the remarkable increase in human power and freedom has inclined modern men to deny and to defy these fixed limits. The tendency to overestimate the degree of increase of human freedom expresses itself most characteristically in the belief that the development of human capacities radically alters the human situation. The final form of the modern error about history is the belief that man's ambiguous position as both a creature and a creator of history is gradually changed until he may, in the foreseeable future, become the unequivocal master of historical destiny. This final and most absurd form of *Hybris* persuades modern culture to reject all Biblical concepts of divine providence as expressions of human impotence and ignorance, no longer relevant to the modern man's situation of intelligence and power.[36]

Thus it is not only on the basis of faulty anthropology that Niebuhr criticizes liberal thought but also with regard to its view of history as redemptive.

Related to the view of history that suggests that life can be harmonized with life in history is a faith in humanity's rational capacity to create community. Niebuhr rejects that excessive faith in rationality when he writes:

Efforts to create world community through world government by constitutional enactment are the consequences of convictions, in a highly mobile and fluid modern culture, that laws and constitutions create communities when it is obvious that they can only strengthen and slightly modify what more unconscious factors have created. These illusions are particularly powerful in America for our own peculiar history encourages the idea that we constituted ourself as a nation through the covenant of the constitution.[37]

The artifact of the U.S. Constitution seemed to suggest to Americans that if a rationally correct document could be devised, community could be created. American experience, or at least the American understanding of that experience, tends to obscure the organic factors that led to a pre-constitutional community.

These three major themes, along with Niebuhr's emphasis on power, the balance of power, and the national interest, make it difficult for hope to be found for activism. It is here that Niebuhr turns to the resources of the Christian tradition. Certainly the thrust of his anthropology and view of history and community make it difficult to find hope in any simple way.

Christians need not succumb to either cynicism or sentimentality. The myth of the Christian faith can prevent a person from falling into despair.

> Christians ought to be able to analyze a given situation more realistically than moralists and idealists because they are not under the necessity of having illusions about human nature in order to avert despair and preserve their faith in the meaning of life. But it is equally true that they are unable to regard any of the pragmatic policies of politics by which relative justice is achieved in history as ultimately normative. This means that Christians always live in a deeper dimension than the realm in which the political struggle takes place. But they cannot simply flee the world of political contention into a realm of mystic eternity or moralistic illusion.[38]

Here Niebuhr is clearly articulating his belief that religious faith can sustain the quest for stability and justice in international relations. The Christian tradition for Reinhold Niebuhr is not a hindrance to the formation of foreign policy. Minorities within the national community, most important to the church, can encourage an idealism that points beyond a narrow national interest, and a realism that reveals the pretense in every effort to transcend the national interest.[39]

In a way that activists, who are not directly responsible for government policy, may fail to appreciate, Niebuhr's realism was Christian in that it held together the poles of idealism and realism. Larry Rasmussen makes two points about how Niebuhr's realism was "Christian":

> (1) Christian realism always meant the interplay of idealism and realism in Niebuhr's mind. The dialectic of his thought— ideal/real, absolute/relative, eternity/time—is to be seen as early as a 1916 article for *Atlantic*. . . . (2) Moreover, the substance and interplay of Niebuhr's categories are theological. "Christian" as a modifier of "realism" means a sober appraisal of human nature with its propensity to let self-regarding impulses overwhelm other-regarding ones, especially in the life of human communities. Niebuhr learned this from Augustine and the Reformation, as well as from the brutal history of the 1930s and 1940s. "Christian" also

points to our essential nature and its *justitia originalis* (original righteousness), still alive in the marrow of our spirit and revealed in Jesus as well as in the vision of the prophets and poets. To describe this essential nature in the terms of "idealism" is to say too little, but at least it is not less than that. In any event, it qualifies "realism" in a way that must not be overlooked in Niebuhr and sometimes is, usually by persons who have difficulty thinking in the terms of high paradox and duality.[40]

Niebuhr's dialectic might sustain people of faith caught in the ambiguities of public policy formulation even though it might not provide a great catalyst for action. (This is probably true even though Niebuhr himself was a catalyst for action.) In short, one should ask to whom is Niebuhr's position most likely to be addressed. Who is the audience? As noted earlier, in the beginning of *Moral Man and Immoral Society* Niebuhr notes, "Contending factions in a social struggle require morale; and morale is created by the right dogmas, symbols and emotionally potent oversimplifications."[41] Straddling the academic, nongovernmental activist, and policy formulation realms, Niebuhr's thought was too nuanced to create easily the morale he wrote about. In addition, because he operated in all three arenas, people currently dealing in those areas look for useful Niebuhrian insights. As Rasmussen states, people unable to maintain the dualities have unjustly criticized Niebuhr and thus emphasize one pole or the other. It should be added that Niebuhr's concerns are not static. Because of the change in Niebuhr's preoccupations and positions, people emphasizing one period in his work over another might not maintain the dualism that Niebuhr himself did. For this reason I believe Henry May, Margaret Byrne Professor of History Emeritus, at the University of California at Berkeley, is correct in stating that in the late sixties Niebuhr was attacked as a Cold Warrior. Niebuhr had moved toward the middle with *The Children of Light and the Children of Darkness* (1944) and toward a "new, somewhat reluctant patriotism" in *The Irony of American History* (1952).[42]

During this 1944–1952 time period Niebuhr not only articulated a defense of democracy, but he also began an attack on communism that helped lay the foundation for the containment of Soviet communism. The turning point in U.S.-Soviet relations came for Niebuhr in 1946. For him,

"Communism came to be viewed as evil as Nazism, but more dangerous because of its utopian appeal and concomitant ability to subvert opponents from within."[43] Niebuhr's understanding of the power of communism's utopian appeal may have prevented him from addressing the ways in which Soviet communism could differ from that of other nations. Yet it was his understanding that helped make his critique of communism so powerful and thus lent credence to those who said he was a Cold Warrior. From what has been shown of Christian realism, as Niebuhr articulated it, a broadened concept of national interest, since it would include more than mere confrontation, should undermine the argument of those who labeled Niebuhr a Cold Warrior. It seems Niebuhr's critics did not appreciate the content of his position.

Not only has Niebuhr been criticized by liberal internationalists for his role in the Cold War but also for separating ethics from politics. J. E. Hare and Carey Joynt argue that Niebuhr puts *agape* out of touch with politics and thereby impoverishes our notion of justice.[44] As noted above, Robert McElroy finds Niebuhr's anthropology so concerned with the pervasiveness of self-interest as to make it very difficult to see any role for justice in international relations. Because of the dialectic tension in Niebuhr's writing, evaluations of his position may be as subjective as seeing the glass as half empty or half full.

One challenge to realists in general that warrants examination is the theoretical characterization of the international arena as a state of nature. Most often the realist's emphasis on the struggle for power reminds one of Hobbes' state of nature in which independent agents work for security without regard for morality in a perpetual state of war. Even though Hobbes was not writing historically but merely using his theoretical state of nature as a tool of analysis, realists, with their claims to historical grounding, make the world seem to confirm Hobbes's construct. Professor Hedley Bull, as a representative of liberal internationalists, challenges the analogy between such a state of nature and international society on three grounds. First, a Hobbesian state of nature has the individual constantly preoccupied with personal security. States in the international society have, for the most part, sufficient security to develop their economic life. Second, Hobbes's state of nature is characterized by an absence of notions of right and wrong. In the international society, even when states and statesmen act immorally (or illegally) they feel compelled to justify their actions on the basis of commonly articulated values. Third, the state of war of all against all in Hobbes's state of nature is in fact the way justice gets approximated in international society. Thus Bull writes:

> The theorist of international society has sought to deal with this difficulty [of accepting Hobbes's war of all against all] not by denying the ubiquity of war, but by questioning the relevance of the model of the modern state. If sovereign states are understood to form a society of a different sort from that constituted by the modern state—one, in particular, whose operation not merely tolerates certain private uses of force but actually requires them—then the fact of a disposition to war can no longer be regarded as evidence that international society does not exist. Theorists of the law of nations and of the system of balance of power have thus sought to show that war does not indicate the absence of international society, or its breakdown, but can occur as a part of its functioning. Thus some international legal writers have seen in war a means by which the law of international society is enforced by individual members; others have seen in it a means of settling political conflicts. Theorists of the balance of power have seen war as the ultimate means by which threats to the international equilibrium are redressed.[45]

While the international arena may be, as Bull is suggesting, a society simply without government, both the costs associated with recent wars and the potential for nuclear war stimulate interest in changing the way states operate whether or not an international society exists. Even if realists concede to Bull the existence of international society, as it seems Morgenthau and Niebuhr would, they still may continue to affirm their point that international politics is still a struggle for power pervaded by human egoism.

Henry Kissinger acknowledges the importance of morality in setting U.S. foreign policy. Kissinger writes,

> For in international politics our morality and power should not be antithetical. . . . Our tradition and the values of our people ensure that a policy that seeks only to manipulate force would lack all conviction, consistency, and public support.[46]

Kissinger, the well-known realist, makes this point and soon afterward amplifies the point, when writing of human rights he states, "we must know how to implement our convictions and achieve an enhancement of human rights *together* with other national objectives."[47] He finds a pragmatic or utilitarian reason for Carter's promotion of human rights. According to Kissinger,

> The aim of the Carter Administration has been to give the American people, after the traumas of Vietnam and Watergate, a renewed sense of the basic decency of this country, so that they may continue to have the pride and self-confidence to remain actively involved in the world.[48]

Kissinger biographer Walter Isaacson, in writing about a Kissinger speech entitled "The Moral Foundations of Foreign Policy," affirms that the support Kissinger would give for recognizing morality in foreign policy would consistently be qualified by a *but* and "by the end of the speech, the *buts* had clearly won."[49] Kissinger's inability to recognize in more than an abstract way the importance of morality in U.S. foreign policy may be one reason the press identifies him with realpolitik rather than some more moderate form of realism. For this student, Kissinger's analytical clarity and understanding obscures the extent to which he was unable either to articulate American concern for human rights or maintain support for the policy of détente.

The late Charles Frankel, once Professor of Philosophy and Public Affairs at Columbia University, has provided a seven-point critique of realism that, if answered successfully, can clarify the strengths as well as the weaknesses of realism and help distinguish Christian realism from realism generally. It should be noted that Frankel points out that the most influential spokesmen for the realists were George Kennan, Hans Morgenthau, and Reinhold Niebuhr. Frankel writes:

> Yet the realists in foreign affairs . . . represent not a tight doctrine but an approach, a convergence of attitudes. They represent indeed the feeling that the realities of international relations are too complex and elusive to be caught by any doctrine. Nevertheless, seven major themes and guiding principles can be discerned in their writings and statements, which allow us to indicate the main drift of their position.[50]

His first point is that realism sees general principles in foreign policy as suspect. While Frankel concedes, "Taken as a warning against over-generalization and over-commitment, this is sound and necessary advice," he then goes on to write, "Taken as a positive recommendation for conducting foreign affairs of a powerful modern state, it fails on the grounds of unrealism."[51] The gist of this criticism is that without general principles there will not be the element of predictability necessary for interstate interaction, and that without general principles a foreign policy will not garner the necessary domestic support. Additionally, the agents of policy themselves need general principles. The realist response to this is not to encourage anarchy among states but base the security of interaction, to the extent security can exist, on what might be termed a general principle of national interest. That is, insofar as interstate interaction is characterized by stability and predictability, that predictability is based on recognizing that nations act on the basis of national interest. While it is not always clear what a nation's interest is, to a significant extent most nations seem agreed on the need for stability, for example, as manifested in diplomatic exchange. In fact, as noted earlier, Hans Morgenthau has described, in his classic work, *Politics among Nations*, six principles of political realism that would provide policymakers with guidelines for making policy that would meet two of Frankel's objections, namely, the need for security in interstate action and the need to provide agents with policy principles upon which to act. On the need for domestic public support for foreign policy, one must acknowledge that some forms of realism in particular might not easily generate public support. As has been pointed out with regard to U.S. foreign policy, because of American concern for morality in its policy there have been swings from isolationism to interventionism. Yet it should be remembered it was the Christian realist Reinhold Niebuhr who, according to President Carter, influenced him, and it was President Carter who won widespread American support for his human rights policy. George Kennan as well encourages some general principles when he recognizes that America, in being true to itself, must be an example to and supporter of *but not a guarantor* of another nation's democracy.[52] Thus this criticism of realism by Frankel seems a bit exaggerated.

The second point in Frankel's critique centers on realism's view that "(t)he enunciation of moral principles in foreign policy contexts encourages zealotry and utopianism."[53] He states:

> What makes moral principles irresponsible is their enunciation without regard to putting them into practice, or to their consequences if acted upon, or to their coherence with other moral principles if acted upon, or to their coherence with other moral principles to which attention also has to be given. In other words, what makes moral principles dangerous is their treatment as absolutes, their immunization from criticism in the light of facts and possibilities. But it is no solution to this problem to suggest, "Look only at the facts; moral principles are distractions." Shorn of their aura of mystery and sanctimony, moral principles are simply guidelines to action. They help us to decide what to do. They are *moral*, not merely technical or pragmatic, because they help us to decide what to do not about evanescent or intermediate matters but about dearly prized values in which our civilization has deep investments and our own sense of identity and self-respect is involved. It is hard to believe that the realists have counseled the extrusion of moral considerations in this sense of the term. What they have wished to extrude, it may be assumed, is moral absolutism. It is not helpful to pursue this objective by what can be too easily construed as a general denigration of the value of moral principles to foreign policy.[54]

From the perspective of Christian realism this criticism seems like a difference in emphasis. As mentioned in relation to the difference between Niebuhr and Morgenthau, Christian realism tends to see a greater role for morality than other forms of realism. Stated pragmatically rather than theoretically, one's own national interest is enhanced by appreciating the interests of other nations. For example, arms control agreements are based on the assumption that, since there probably is no absolute security a nation can guarantee for itself unilaterally, those agreements are most likely to be effective which take into account the enhancement of security for all parties to an agreement (otherwise there would be little incentive for a nation to join or adhere to the agreement).

Frankel's third criticism of realism addresses what he sees as the realist preference for genuine working understandings over dramatic agreements on paper. Frankel critiques realism by qualifying this realist preference in two ways. First, Frankel argues the realist needs to take into account the increasing role of nongovernmental actors, as distinct from diplomats, in the international arena. Second, he argues that the realist must understand, "The evolution of working understandings along a broad spectrum of transnational activities is indeed the substance of progress in foreign affairs."[55] Without exaggerating the progress to be made, it seems clear that Niebuhr himself recognized the role and value of nongovernmental activities particularly with regard to his own activities with and appreciation for the United Nations Educational Scientific and Cultural Organization.[56] Frankel's fourth criticism of realism is its emphasis on professionalism in foreign policy. Yet in amplifying this criticism he writes, "professional diplomats often know foreign countries better than their own and lack the powers of communication to touch base effectively with the citizenry at home."[57] Additionally, Frankel writes, "the translation of respect for professionalism into an operative governmental policy is that the professionals do not themselves perform as a unified group with a common judgment."[58] Yet these criticisms are not really against professionalism in foreign policy but rather problems requiring better communications among foreign policy professionals and between those professionals and their home countries.

Frankel's fifth criticism deals with the realist's dichotomy between morals and politics. He writes:

> The realist states a general truth which applies to far more than foreign policy. That truth is that the moral rules that apply to people performing complex social roles are not the same as those applying to people in their more intimate personal or familial relations. . . . But this truth is obscured when it is stated as a conflict between the realm of morals and the non-moral realm of politics. What is involved is a collision between different sets of moral rules, not the extrusion of morality from one domain. A major source of this confusion is the unstated presupposition that morality or ethics stand only for the traditional maxims of face-to-face relations. . . . This habit of restricting the meaning of morality to a narrow and traditional frame is a major obstacle to the humane improvement of complex social institutions. . . . International affairs are simply a particularly pertinent and poignant illustration of the problem of resolving conflicts of moral

standards. They are not a domain where people have no choice but to be immoral.[59]

It seems clear that Niebuhr does not separate politics from morality, and certainly he does not equate morality with traditional maxims of face-to-face relations. Although Niebuhr does say that justice is to be judged in light of the absolute virtue of sacrificial love (which most clearly was expressed in the death of Jesus), he clearly states that justice in terms of collectivities is something other than the love which is the ideal in interpersonal relations. Thus Niebuhr writes:

> There is an ecstatic form of agape which defines the ultimate heroic possibilities of human existence (involving, of course, martyrdom) but not the common possibilities of tolerable harmony of life with life. In so far as justice admits the claims of the self, it is something less than love. Yet it cannot exist without love and remain justice. For without the "grace" of love, justice always degenerates into something less than justice. But if justice requires that the interests of the self be entertained, it also requires that they be resisted. Every realistic system of justice must assume the continued power of self-interest, particularly of collective self-interest.[60]

Morgenthau too, though less explicitly than Niebuhr, sees morality and politics related, in such a way as to paradoxically support Frankel's position that what actually exists is a different set of moral standards which at the same time tie morality to politics. In this regard Morgenthau writes:

> Man is a political animal by nature; he is a scientist by chance or choice; he is a moralist because he is a man. Man is born to seek power, yet his actual condition makes him a slave to the power of others. Man is born a slave, but everywhere he wants to be a master. Out of this discord between man's desire and his actual condition arises the moral issue of power, that is, the problem of justifying and limiting the power which man has over man. Hence, the history of political thought is the history of the moral evaluation of political power, and the scientism of Machiavelli and Hobbes is, in the history of mankind, merely an accident without consequences, a sudden flash of lightning illuminating

the dark landscape of man's hidden motives but kindling no Promethean fire for a grateful posterity. Even when mankind seems to be preoccupied with the science of man's political nature and considers ethics either as an empirical science or considers it not at all, the moral issues raise their voices and demand an answer. The answers, like the questions, are mumbled, ambiguous, and distorted when scientific prejudices do not allow the moral problems to be seen in their true light and the answers to be given in their true relation to the questions. Thus it remains for every age, and particularly a scientific one, to rediscover and reformulate the perennial problems of political ethics and to answer them in the light of the experience of the age.[61]

This passage both justifies Frankel's criticism that realism represents a different set of moral standards and denies the criticism that realism necessarily posits politics as a realm unrelated to morality.

It is this criticism of Frankel that is most intriguing. To the extent he is right about different moral standards operating, once that may be acknowledged, discussion between idealists and realists might be possible. For example, even the most profound idealist would concede that the need for national security is a legitimate part of the power drive of which the realists write.

Frankel's sixth criticism deals with the realist assertion that foreign policy should be based on human nature as it is, not as the policymaker would like it to be. This, too, Frankel believes is a good point pushed too far. He criticizes Niebuhr for using the same religious language to criticize Wilsonian idealism as Wilson used to promote it. Thus Frankel suggests a Spinoza-inspired naturalistic discussion of the goodness and evil of mankind in the political arena.[62] Niebuhr's response would be to say that by couching his argument in the language of Christian faith he was reclaiming an orthodox position that stood against the religious position that heretically ignored the depth of human sin and selfishness. By using the language he did he was able to stand against a culturally defined philosophical faith in human progress. The historical grounding of the Christian faith allows it, according to Niebuhr, to stand against a utopian vision that lacked an adequate understanding of human nature. Niebuhr made this argument, among other writings, in his essay "Why The Christian Church Is Not Pacifist."[63]

Prudence, a supreme virtue in policymaking, would require the policymaker to operate under no illusions as to what the other nation's leadership may be capable of doing. For Reinhold Niebuhr an authentic reaffirmation of the insights of the Christian tradition can insolate a person from the optimism and faith in progress likely to distort good judgment. As noted in the preceding chapter, this may be done without requiring everyone to be Christian or even religious.

Frankel's last criticism of realism is that realism's emphasis on international relations as rivalry-relations and foreign policy as the pursuit of national interest prevents the policymaker, and others, from seeing how other relationships might exist to bring about more desirable forms of interaction. To illuminate this criticism Frankel quotes David Hume to the effect that philosophers, attempting to hold no illusions about human nature, who overemphasize selfishness in human nature do not take into account how such things as love of family, desire for the respect of others, and concern for the institutions of society mitigate against the effects of selfishness. Realists, according to Frankel, pay too little attention to other positive variables.[64]

This critique of realism, even Niebuhrian realism, may seem justified, as is noted above, for example, in McElroy's complaint that there seemed to be little hope in Niebuhr's thought, but for two exceptions. First, Niebuhr recognizes how it is in the national interest to take into account the interest of other nations, and therefore to be less rigorously self-interested. Second, Niebuhr's emphasis on the possibility of justice, even at the international level, would minimize the negative effects of pursuit of the national interest. Niebuhr's concern over the self-interestedness of nations is expressed in his concern that nations claim more sacred status than they deserve. The tendency toward idolatry must be held in check. In a passage that could apply to the end of the Cold War as well as the end of World War II, Niebuhr writes:

Consider our relations to our vanquished enemies. We were certainly righteous when we fought the Nazis, that is, righteous by comparison. But how quickly our righteousness runs out, not only because we have destroyed the evil with which we compared ourselves, but also because we inherited some of the irresponsible power through our victory, which tainted them with evil.[65]

This preoccupation with the nation's sense of its own virtue even at the end of a righteous war mitigates against a too narrow self-interest that Frankel criticizes. Even more explicitly Niebuhr writes:

> Since their (nations') ultimate interests are always protected best, by at least a measure of fairness toward their neighbors, the desire to gain an immediate selfish advantage always imperils their ultimate interests.[66]

This perspective in Niebuhr's thought might be overlooked because of his preoccupation with addressing how the United States should deal with authoritarianism of both the right and left. Nevertheless, one should not conclude that Niebuhr did not write of international relations in terms of rivalry or foreign policy in terms of national interest.

Frankel's criticisms, at least with regard to Christian realism, either tend to exaggerate the points made by realism or neglect to take into account other mitigating positions taken by realism. This is not to suggest that Frankel's concerns need not be addressed, in fact such concerns might serve to prevent realism from making the errors Frankel suggests.

In light of the particular subject matter of this work, promotion of human rights, it should be noted that arguments from either the realist positions (i.e., either secular or Christian) or the moralistic legalistic position could encourage a foreign policy promoting human rights. There is nothing intrinsic to the realist argument that would prevent realists from encouraging a strong pro-human rights policy. That is so because it could be in the national interest to want human rights to be recognized. The case has been made that promotion of human rights via the CSCE contributed to the breakup of the Soviet Empire and the Soviet Union itself, a goal many, perhaps most, American foreign policy realists favored.

Moralists, of either the right or left, would generally favor foreign policies promoting human rights. In fact we have seen moralists of both persuasions arguing in favor of aggressive human rights policies. The difference between the realists and the moralists is that the former might be reluctant because of the need to exist side-by-side with the other countries, and the complexities of the issues make them humble. The moralists would have been more likely to encourage a vigorous stance because of the moral norms involved, and perhaps less prudent about the costs of such a policy.

Morality and Foreign Policy

The debate between realists and idealists has obscured, among other things, the role of morality in realist theory. As has been noted, for the realist the moral character of policy is seen very largely in the consequences of the policy. While this no doubt strikes some as simply a case of the end justifying the means, it is a legitimate ethical perspective. The role of morality as an ideological support for policy in realist theory has also been noted. In addition the Christian realism of Reinhold Niebuhr posits morality in defining the concept of national interest in such a way as to take into account the interests of other nations. Even in the writing of Hans Morgenthau one finds morality playing a role to moderate the competition among the monarchies of seventeenth, eighteenth, and nineteenth-century Europe. Thus Morgenthau describes the European princes and aristocratic rulers as sharing "common moral convictions about what a gentleman was and was not allowed to do in his relations with another gentleman, whether of his own or of a foreign nation."[67] Consequently, Morgenthau in his criticism of moralism in setting foreign policy laments the lack of moral consensus that characterized Europe prior to World War I. He writes:

> This fragmentation of a formerly cohesive international society into a multiplicity of morally self-sufficient national communities, which have ceased to operate within a common framework of moral precepts, is but the outward symptom of the profound change that in recent times has transformed the relations between universal moral precepts and the particular systems of national ethics. The transformation has proceeded in two different ways. It has weakened, to the point of ineffectiveness, the universal, supranational moral rules of conduct, which before the age of nationalism had imposed a system—however precarious and wide-meshed—of limitations upon the foreign policies of individual nations. Conversely, it has greatly strengthened the tendency of individual nations to endow their particular national system of ethics with universal validity.[68]

Thus it would be a mistake to argue that Morgenthau simply rails against morality in international relations. Morgenthau is arguing against moralism in foreign policy. Even two of his critics write,

> A charitable interpretation of the "realists" like Hans Morgenthau and George Kennan is that they are advising American diplomats to err on the side of power politics because they have been too prone in the past to err on the side of a moralistic idealism.[69]

This statement seem to imply a morality in Morgenthau's writing, and it is left to the reader to determine how "charitable" one must be to conclude that the realists are merely attempting to avoid an extreme moralistic idealism.

Dr. Roger Shinn, accepting the realist's criticism of moralism in foreign policy, describes four ways in which ethics can enter into policymaking. First, ethics can help policymakers see more clearly the relationship between means and ends. Second, a concern with morality can enhance the emphasis on the role of diplomacy in identifying mutually advantageous solutions to disputes. Third, morality may help policymakers understand more clearly what their real interests are. Fourth, a sensitivity to ethical considerations increases the likelihood of understanding the ethical component within the national interest.[70] Proximate goals sought through values prudently expressed and formulated in a framework like that outlined above can insinuate morality into foreign policy formation. The content of the goals as well as the values relating means to ends and the national interest can be informed by justice. Justice, in turn, is defined by and judged by the Christian understanding of *agape*.

Unfortunately, in practice the above formulation may not be very emotionally satisfying. It is for that reason that Christian realism is only one of three basic religious outlooks on foreign policy. According to Earl Brill, in addition to Christian realism there is a "moralistic patriotism" and an "idealistic-humanitarian" approach. The "moralistic patriotism" is often associated with evangelical Protestantism, but it is also shared by religious liberals who encourage a Wilsonian interventionism. In this approach America is to advance the cause of freedom. For the evangelicals, to be a good Christian is to be a good American. In this way of thinking the United States has been chosen by God to bring to the rest of the world the benefits of Christianity, democracy, and the capitalist system.[71]

The "idealistic-humanitarian" approach is pro-UN and tends to be multilateral. It judges foreign policy by universal moral standards.

> Thus the goals of foreign policy should be the Christian virtues of peace, justice, equality, human rights, and the rule of law. Foreign governments are judged to be good or evil according to their commitment to these values. American policy should support the good and disassociate from the evil. Dictators are generally condemned and revolutions of the people supported.[72]

(This statement reveals, as will be seen in the last chapter, how at odds with realism this "idealistic-humanitarian" approach is.)

Both of these approaches encourage the promotion of human rights. To the extent that the United Nations, or any other multilateral institution, is an instrument of U.S. policy, both religious approaches might converge. Yet in addition to "moralistic patriotism" and "idealistic-humanitarianism" there is Christian realism.

The benefits of the Christian realism of Reinhold Niebuhr are numerous. An awareness of Christian realism's emphasis on the organic prerequisites of community prevents a premature reliance on and utopian expectations of the United Nations. Realism recognizes the moral ambiguity associated with policy and therefore inhibits extravagant claims being made by the nation. By recognizing the lack of control over the direction of history, realism promotes the virtue of prudence. Christian realism, because it draws on the resources of faith, helps people develop the discipline necessary for activism in the face of ambiguity and paradox. It helps policymakers choose responsibly among tragic alternatives knowing that with God's grace even without a pure heart one can and must act.

From what has been said about "moralistic patriotism" it should be clear that, in relation to Brill's schema, the two categories this chapter is concerned with are Christian realism and "idealistic-humanitarianism." That there is a role for morality in foreign policy, according to the mainline Protestant churches, will be illustrated in the examination of their involvement in the policy formation process. That those same churches may use elements of Christian realism and "idealistic-humanitarianism" may be less clear. As we have seen it is possible for both approaches to support the same policy. In the following chapter it will be seen how human rights might easily have been supported from either position (though the difficulty inherent in promoting human rights via Christian realism will be noted).

In summary, there is a role for Christian ethics in the formation of foreign policy. It is a role that eschews moralism and the temptation to make one's self and one's nation righteous through foreign policy actions. The role is one that seeks to promote a national interest that takes into account the legitimate interests of other nations. It is a role that attempts to inform the nation and other nations of the content of justice, as the Christian tradition informs that concept. Finally, Christian ethics should help us to understand our own nation's limitations and mistakes.

Notes

1. Roger L. Shinn, "Realism and Ethics in Political Philosophy," in *A Tribute to Hans Morgenthau*, with an Intellectual Autobiography by Hans J. Morgenthau, ed. Kenneth Thompson and Robert J. Myers with the assistance of Robert Osgood and Tang Tsou (Washington, D.C.: The New Republic Book Company, Inc., 1977), 95.

2. Joseph S. Nye Jr., *Nuclear Ethics* (N.Y.: The Free Press, 1980), 20.

3. Hoffmann, *Duties beyond Borders: On the Limits and Possibilities of Ethical International Relations* (Syracuse, N.Y.: Syracuse University Press, 1998), 17-19.

4. Niebuhr, *Moral Man and Immoral Society: A Study in Ethics and Politics* (N.Y.: Charles Scribner's Sons, 1960) , 257, 263, 267-68.

5. Robert W. McElroy, *Morality and American Foreign Policy: The Role of Ethics in International Affairs* (Princeton, N.J.: Princeton University Press, 1992), 5.

6. McElroy, *Morality and American Foreign Policy*, 8-11.

7. McElroy, *Morality and American Foreign Policy*, 12-13.

8. Rene Albrecht-Carrie, *A Diplomatic History of Europe since the Congress of Vienna* (N.Y.: Harper and Brothers Publishers, 1958), 375-77.

9. Immanuel Kant, "Eternal Peace," in *The Philosophy of Kant: Immanuel Kant's Moral and Political Writings,* ed. Carl J. Friedrich (N.Y.: The Modern Library, 1977), 443.

10. Kant, "Eternal Peace," 453.

11. Kant, "Eternal Peace," 436.

12. Kant, "Eternal Peace," 80.

13. Inis L. Claude Jr., *Power and International Relations* (N.Y.: Random House, 1969), 85.

14. Woodrow Wilson, *The Public Papers of Woodrow Wilson, War and Peace,* ed. Ray S. Baker and William E. Dodd (N.Y.: Harper, 1927), II, 234, 235, quoted in Claude, *Power and International Relations,* 82.

15. The assertion of Morgenthau's standing in the academic community is based on the widespread use of his book *Politics among Nations* as the text for introductory courses in international relations.

16. Hans J. Morgenthau, *Scientific Man vs. Power Politics* (Chicago: University of Chicago Press, 1974; reprint, Chicago: University of Chicago Press, 1946), 203.

17. Morgenthau and Thompson, *Politics among Nations: The Struggle for Power and Peace,* 6th ed. (N.Y.: McGraw-Hill Publishing Company, 1985), 45.

18. Morgenthau and Thompson, *Politics among Nations,* 10, 12.

19. Morgenthau and Thompson, *Politics among Nations,* 13.

20. McElroy, *Morality and American Foreign Policy,* 23.

21. Morgenthau and Thompson, *Politics among Nations,* 12.

22. Hans J. Morgenthau, "National Interest and Moral Principles in Foreign Policy: The Primacy of the National Interest," *American Scholar* XVIII (Spring, 1949), 207, 211 quoted in Robert C. Good, "The National Interest and Political Realism: Niebuhr's 'Debate' with Morgenthau and Kennan," *Journal of Politics* 22 (November 1960), 602.

23. Hans J. Morgenthau, originally quoted in Norman Podhoretz, *Why We Were in Vietnam* (N.Y.: Simon and Schuster, 1982), 105, from Henry Kissinger, *Diplomacy* (N.Y.: Simon and Schuster, 1994), 668.

24. Good, "The National Interest and Political Realism: Niebuhr's 'Debate' with Morgenthau and Kennan," 609.

25. Good, "The National Interest and Political Realism: Niebuhr's 'Debate' with Morgenthau and Kennan," 604-5.

26. Shinn, "Realism and Ethics in Political Philosophy," 95.

27. Good, "The National Interest and Political Realism: Niebuhr's 'Debate' with Morgenthau and Kennan," 610-11.

28. Kenneth W. Thompson, *Christian Ethics and the Dilemmas of Foreign Policy* (Durham, N.C.: Duke University Press, 1959), 17.

29. Reinhold Niebuhr, *The Children of Light and the Children of Darkness: A Vindication of Democracy and a Critique of Its Traditional Defense* (N.Y.: Charles Scribner's Sons, 1966), 20.

30. Niebuhr, *The Children of Light*, 41.

31. Niebuhr, *Moral Man and Immoral Society*, 4.

32. McElroy, *Morality and American Foreign Policy*, 16.

33. Reinhold Niebuhr, *Christianity and Power Politics* (N.Y.: Archon Books, 1969; reprint, N.Y.: Charles Scribner's Sons, 1940), ixx.

34. Niebuhr, *Christianity and Power Politics*, 45.

35. Niebuhr, *Christianity and Power Politics*, 5.

36. Niebuhr, *Faith and History*, 70.

37. Reinhold Niebuhr, *The Structure of Nations and Empires: A Study of the Recurring Patterns and Problems of the Political Order in Relation to the Unique Problems of the Nuclear Age* (N.Y.: Charles Scribner's Sons, 1959), 262.

38. Reinhold Niebuhr, "A Christian Peace Policy," *Radical Religion* (Spring), 1939, 11, quoted in *Reinhold Niebuhr on Politics: His Political Philosophy and Its Application to Our Age as Expressed in His Writings* ed. H. R. Davis and R. C. Good (N.Y.: Charles Scribner's Sons, 1960), 193-97, quoted in Rasmussen, *Reinhold Niebuhr: Theologian of Public Life*,130.

39. Good, "The National Interest and Political Realism; Niebuhr's 'Debate' with Morgenthau and Kennan," 619.

40. Rasmussen, *Reinhold Niebuhr: Theologian of Public Life*, 21-22.

41. Niebuhr, *Moral Man and Immoral Society*, xv.

42. May, *The Divided Heart: Essays on Protestantism and the Enlightenment in America*, 21, 23-24, 66.

43. Russell Foster Sizemore, "Reinhold Niebuhr and the Rhetoric of Liberal Anti-Communism: Christian Realism and the Rise of the Cold War," Ph.D. diss., Harvard University, 1987, 115.

44. J. E. Hare and Carey B. Joynt, *Ethics and International Affairs* (N.Y.: St. Martin's Press, 1982), 33.

45. Hedley Bull, "Society and Anarchy in International Relations," in *Conflict after the Cold War: Arguments on Causes of War and Peace*, ed. Richard K. Betts (N.Y.: Macmillan Publishing Company, 1994), 140-41. A similar point on the international society and how it contrasts with Hobbes's state of nature is made by Charles R. Beitz in *Political Theory and International Relations* (Princeton, N.J.: Princeton University Press, 1979).

46. Henry Kissinger, "Continuity and Change in American Foreign Policy," in *Human Rights and World Order*, ed. Abdul Aziz Said (New Brunswick, N. J.: Transaction Books, 1978), 159.

47. Kissinger, "Continuity and Change in American Foreign Policy," 160.

48. Kissinger, "Continuity and Change in American Foreign Policy."

49. Walter Isaccson, *Kissinger: A Biography* (N.Y.: Simon & Schuster, 1992), 660.

50. Charles Frankel, "Morality and U.S. Foreign Policy," in *Private and Public Ethics: Tensions between Conscience and Institutional Responsibility*, ed. Donald G. Jones (N.Y.: The Edwin Mellon Press, 1978), 69-70.

51. Frankel, "Morality and U.S. Foreign Policy," 73.

52. George F. Kennan, "On American Principles," *Foreign Affairs* 74 (March-April 1995): 118, 124.

53. Frankel, "Morality and U.S. Foreign Policy," 76.

54. Frankel, "Morality and U.S. Foreign Policy," 77.

55. Frankel, "Morality and U.S. Foreign Policy," 80.

56. Ronald H. Stone, *Professor Reinhold Niebuhr: A Mentor to the Twentieth Century* (Louisville, Ky.: Westminster/John Knox Press, 1973), 242-43.

57. Frankel, "Morality and U.S. Foreign Policy," 81.

58. Frankel, "Morality and U.S. Foreign Policy," 82.

59. Frankel, "Morality and U.S. Foreign Policy," 82-84.

60. Reinhold Niebuhr, *Love and Justice: Selections from the Shorter Writings of Reinhold Niebuhr*, ed. D. B. Robertson (Louisville, Ky.: Westminster/John Knox Press, 1957), 28.

61. Morgenthau, *Scientific Man vs. Power Politics*, 168-69.

62. Frankel, "Morality and U.S. Foreign Policy," 86-88.

63. Reinhold Niebuhr, *The Essential Reinhold Niebuhr*, ed. Robert McAfee Brown (New Haven, Conn.: Yale University Press, 1986), 104-5.

64. Frankel, "Morality and U.S. Foreign Policy," 89-90.

65. Niebuhr, *Love and Justice*, 162.

66. Niebuhr, *Moral Man and Immoral Society*, 86.

67. Morgenthau and Thompson, *Politics among Nations*, 261.

68. Morgenthau and Thompson, *Politics among Nations*, 268-69.

69. Hare and Joynt, *Ethics and International Affairs*, 7.

70. Shinn, "Realism and Ethics in Political Philosophy," 100-3.

71. Earl H. Brill, "Religious Influences on United States Foreign Policy," in *American Character and Foreign Policy*, ed. Michael P. Hamilton (Grand Rapids, Mich.: William B. Eerdmans Publishing Company, 1986), 61.

72. Brill, "Religious Influences on United States Foreign Policy," 62.

Chapter 3

The Protestant Churches and Human Rights

This chapter focuses on the attempt of Protestant churches to influence U.S. human rights policy, particularly with regard to the CSCE process from 1973 to 1980. Because of its Protestant constituency and its usefulness to that constituency in appearing to witness for Protestant communions, the activities of the National Council of Churches of Christ (NCCC) will be particularly significant for an understanding of how the Protestant churches sought to influence policy. Reference will be made as well to the role of the World Council of Churches.

In evaluating the role of the Protestant churches this chapter will address several questions. How did the churches attempt to influence policy regarding human rights in the Helsinki Accord? To what extent did the rationales presented by the churches echo concerns that might be raised from a Christian realist perspective? What are the theological rationales underlying the human rights provisions of the churches? In answering these questions we will be able to outline the problems associated with relating morality to setting foreign policy. In addition we will see some characteristic features of U.S. foreign policy development.

Church Interaction with the Government

Congress, of the three branches of our national government, is the primary focus for church lobbying activities. The judiciary is the least involved in foreign policy formulation and, therefore, the one least likely to be approached by interest groups. That certainly is the case in the present policy under discussion. While one might expect groups, such as churches, to attempt to influence the executive directly, since it has major responsibility for setting and executing foreign policy, for four reasons this was not the case. First, during much of the time from 1973 to 1980 access to the president was limited (this is particularly true during the Nixon administration from 1973 to 1975).[1] Second, the bureaucratic formulation of policy makes it difficult to identify effective points of contact. Third, the congressional initiative with regard to Helsinki made the legislative branch an even more attractive entry point for human rights groups. Fourth, Congress is the primary target of nonprofit lobbying for human rights since it is linked to public opinion.[2]

With the greater access to Congress noted, the mainline Protestant churches did have some conversations with presidents Ford and Carter during the time period under consideration. The most notable conversation for the purposes of this paper was a meeting initiated by the National Council of Churches of Christ with President Carter. The meeting took place February 24, 1978. The twenty-eight member delegation was led by William P. Thompson, the stated clerk of the United Presbyterian Church and president of the NCC. The meeting was notable not for its dealing directly with human rights but because President Carter took the opportunity to criticize Sunday morning worship as the most segregated hour in the week for Americans.[3] Even though a memo had been sent to President Carter outlining points to discuss (including international human rights policy) prior to the meeting, the president did not address those issues.[4] What seems significant here is that President Carter, meeting with a presumably supportive group, did not stress human rights policy, which had been so central to his foreign policy.

In terms of Congress, the preferred arena for human rights groups to articulate their positions, a review of the Congressional Information Service Cumulative Index for 1975 to 1978 reveals that the National

Council of Churches of Christ testified before Congress thirty-two times in those years, and in nine times the testimony dealt with human rights. Upon examination one finds that only on one occasion did testimony deal with human rights in Europe and then only peripherally. The other statements before congressional bodies dealt with human rights violations in Haiti, Nicaragua, El Salvador, Guatemala, South Korea, Vietnam, the Democratic People's Republic of Korea, South Africa, and Chile.

In the same vein, during the period from 1975 to 1978 the United Methodist Church testified before Congress on human rights in Brazil, India, and South Korea; the United Church of Christ testified on human rights in Indonesia, the Philippines, and Romania. The Episcopal Churchmen spoke to Congress on human rights in South Africa.

Subsequent CIS indexes covering 1979 and 1980 indicate the same trend of NCCC testimony or testimony by mainline Protestant churches addressing human rights in non-European countries. In 1979 the NCCC did testify in hearings before the Senate Foreign Relations committee on the need for the United States to ratify human rights treaties.

In *Human Rights & World Politics*, David Forsythe examines nonprofit human rights advocacy groups and their role in "Humanizing American Foreign Policy," and the examples of the NCCC or related churches' activities tend to confirm the emphasis on violations in countries of Asia, Africa, and Latin America.[5] Perhaps neglect of Western European countries' human rights activities should be neither surprising nor of great concern, but certainly that is not the case with East European countries. Yet even so, the neglect of Eastern Europe was not complete, for Forsythe cites one midlevel State Department official as saying, "Nonprofit criticism of our (U.S.) performance at the Belgrade meeting under the Helsinki Accord is going to make the United States tougher at the Madrid meeting."[6] (This statement is made in the context of a discussion of church-sponsored organizations, as well as other non-profits.)

Claire Randall, at the time general secretary of the National Council of Churches of Christ in the U.S.A., in testimony before the Senate Foreign Relations Committee on January 21, 1976, spoke about "siding with the powerless" by withdrawing U.S. support for repressive governments. In this section of her testimony Dr. Randall states,

[S]urely the most effective way to promote democracy and oppose communism is to support those activities of other nations which build a decent standard of living and political freedom for all persons. Détente has helped us to understand it is possible for nations with opposing ideologies to work together for common goals. It is a mockery to speak of self-determination while overtly or covertly supporting regimes which deny liberty to their citizens and frustrate legitimate desires of the people.[7]

The perspective here is clearly to articulate the position that U.S. foreign policy ought not support repressive regimes, and she specifically cites South Africa, Rhodesia, South Korea, the Philippines, and Chile, while omitting any direct reference to the Soviet Union. In this statement it seems as if Dr. Randall is saying that détente and the promotion of human rights are complementary rather than contradictory. Dr. Randall goes on in the human rights section of her testimony to say:

In recent years we have seen an increase in the violation of human rights in many parts of the world. We deplore these violations in whatever country they occur, but we are filled with shame at the degree to which the United States government has provided economic, military, and political support to some of the most flagrant violators.[8]

Even in this human rights portion of the testimony the focus is on non-European states.

There were probably several explanations for not discussing human rights violations by East European countries in the testimony. Dr. Randall, aware of how U.S. policy aids repressive regimes, would naturally be reluctant to criticize the policies of the Soviet Union for fear of generating American self-righteousness. In addition, since the U.S. government would have more influence vis à vis the governments mentioned than those of Eastern Europe, perhaps she thought she should talk about the area in which U.S. policy changes could be most effective. It is likely that since the Helsinki Accord had been signed only six months prior to this testimony, neither she nor other members of the mainline Protestant churches realized the potential importance of the agreement's human rights provisions. Another possible explanation for this omission is the desire to maintain détente between the United States and Soviet Union.

Related to the last reason is the desire of the NCCC to maintain ties with the Russian Orthodox Church. (It should be noted that this testimony occurred after the World Council of Churches at their Nairobi Assembly discussed extensively the human rights provisions of the Helsinki Accord, especially with regard to religious liberty.)

One observer of the NCCC puts the organization's attitude toward the Soviet Union and Eastern Europe in the context of its relationship with the churches this way:

> [T]he Council also has relationships, albeit of a different kind (than with the Third World), with the official churches of Eastern Europe and the Soviet Union. Although initially sharing in the anti-Communist sentiment of the early 1950s, the National Council of Churches sought in the 1960s and more recently to build positive relationships with the Soviet Union, by establishing friendly ties with the Russian Orthodox Church and the officially recognized churches of Eastern Europe and by helping church members in the United States to have a more appreciative understanding of the people and cultures of Communist countries. The changing flavor of official pronouncements by the Council through the 1960s and early 1970s reflects a disavowal of "cold war" hostility toward the Soviet Union as well as a growing disenchantment with United States policy and culture under the impact of Vietnam, Watergate, and the floundering of the civil rights movement in the northern U.S. cities.[9]

An additional reason for NCCC (and WCC) reluctance to criticize Soviet human rights violations, suggested by George Will in Ernest Lefever's *Amsterdam to Nairobi: The World Council of Churches and the Third World*, was the supposed leftist nature of the councils. (This was also a thesis of commentaries in *Reader's Digest* and on the popular television news program *60 Minutes*.) It goes beyond the scope of this study to assess the validity of this charge, but the criticism should be noted.

Nevertheless, as the testimony of Dr. Randall makes clear, the NCCC was concerned with human rights. A year later in a letter to President-elect Jimmy Carter the National Council of Churches along with eight other organizations continued to press for human rights, but once again in relation to the issue of U.S. security assistance.[10]

In 1977 the NCCC created its Human Rights Office under the leadership of William L. Wipfler, formerly head of the NCCC's Latin America Office.[11] Representing the NCCC, Mr. Wipfler testified to the Senate Foreign Relations Committee in 1979 in support of U.S. ratification of several human rights treaties.[12]

In the preceding chapter it was noted that it was the West Europeans who provided the impetus for including forceful human rights provisions in the Final Act. Now we will find that it is out of the context of the World Council of Churches that a program was developed to lift up the human rights provisions of the Accord. As we have seen in regard to Helsinki and U.S. Protestant churches little appeal was made to Congress between the time the Accord was signed and 1981. Even so the World Council of Churches explored with European and North American church leaders possibilities of cooperating on human rights. As a consequence the Canadian Council of Churches, the Conference of European Churches, and the National Council of Churches by 1979 formally agreed to sponsor jointly the Churches' Human Rights Programme for the Implementation of the Helsinki Final Act.[13]

The evolution of concern over human rights within the WCC predated the signing of the Helsinki Accord. "In 1974, an important consultation 'Human Rights and Christian Responsibility' was organized by the WCC in St. Polten, Austria."[14] Some of the most intense discussions of the issues of human rights and particularly religious liberty took place at the Fifth Assembly of the WCC in 1975 in Nairobi. At Nairobi the Russian Orthodox Church, supported by the East European churches, defended "the evolution of democratic principles under socialism against those who . . . wanted a resolution from the WCC condemning the Soviet Union."[15] Of course the WCC picked up on Principle VII of the Final Act, which, among other things, provides for the participating states to respect "human rights and fundamental freedoms, including freedom of thought, conscience, religion or belief, for all without distinction as to race, sex, language or religion. . . ."[16] The WCC followed up on the discussions at Nairobi by circulating approximately 1,000 copies of the Accord to church leaders in Europe, and by organizing meetings at Montreux and Geneva on aspects of religious liberty.[17] The activity of the WCC for human rights has led Max Stackhouse, Professor of Christian Ethics at Princeton Theological Seminary, to assert that the WCC "has done more for human rights among the peoples of the world than any other single international body."[18] Max Stackhouse, a well-known critic of the WCC, made this positive comment in the midst of a general criticism of the WCC.

For the purposes of discussion in this chapter it should be kept in mind that "The Churches' Human Rights Programme for the Implementation of the Helsinki Final Act" was begun in 1980 and ended in 1985.[19] Even though that program falls outside the scope of this book, one would find that the most significant efforts of the program lay outside of the realm of U.S. foreign policy formulation. The somewhat nonpolitical (at least in a direct sense) nature of the subsequent WCC activities can be seen in light of a March 1977 meeting of a small ad hoc planning group (comprised of representatives of churches in the USSR, Romania, Italy, Czechoslovakia, the United States, the United Kingdom, and the German Federal Republic) that met to propose:

> a common program of studies for churches on human rights and expressed the desire that such studies would be action-oriented, that representatives of churches in various areas would hold meetings to share the results of their studies, that small working groups would be set up to pursue in-depth studies of particular problems on human rights, that specific bodies would be created within each church and national church council to bear responsibility for programs of study and action on human rights and religious liberty and, finally, that an international consultative body would be organized to ensure the implementation of this plan of ecumenical activities.[20]

Perhaps this lack of political orientation should not be too surprising. An appeal for WCC support had come from two Soviet dissidents to the Nairobi conference, causing criticism of the Soviet Union and an uneasy atmosphere. The Russian Orthodox Church abstained from voting on the final document put before the Nairobi Assembly on "Disarmament-The Helsinki Agreement Religious Liberty." This abstention, as explained by Professor Vitaly Borovoy (a delegate of the Russian Orthodox Church), was a result of the acrimonious atmosphere surrounding the discussion, and the abstention clearly revealed the difficult position the East European churches found themselves in.[21]

As in the discussion of why the NCCC failed to address human rights violations in Eastern Europe, there were probably several reasons why the WCC did not rebuke the Soviet Union. One of the more likely reasons (for both the WCC and the NCCC) for a reticence to be too condemnatory is the realization that all nations have sinned. This is the substance of two statements, one by Mr. Dwain C. Epps (executive secretary for International Affairs, Peace and Human Rights of the WCC and later International Affairs officer of the NCCC) and the other by Dr. William Wipfler (director of the Human Rights Office of the NCCC). In a letter to Rep. Millicent Fenwick (R. N.J.) of the U.S. House of Representatives, who was one of the chief sponsors of a bill establishing the joint House-Senate Commission on the Conference on Security and Cooperation in Europe, Mr. Epps alluded to churches in the United States have pointed out practices in the United States that, in their view, contradicted the Helsinki principles. Mr. Epps stated, as well, the WCC concern that human rights should not be used as an ideological weapon.[22] (Rep. Fenwick attempted to have Mr. Epps be more specific in his charges but was unsuccessful in getting more detail.)

In a similar vein of criticism of the United States, Dr. William Wipfler, in arguing that the United States should ratify human rights treaties, stated:

> I believe that every people is a mythmaking people. We all have myths of one kind or another which help undergird the values of our society. I think the United States is a society that has held a belief in its own justice and to a great degree this is based on the laws to which we can appeal. Nevertheless, we all recognize that during the 1950's, 1960's, and 1970's we have gone through some very difficult and painful struggles in the United States, particularly in the area of racial problems and the rights of minorities. . . . Thus, while we are a mythmaking people concerning the guarantees that we have, almost always setting forth our own system as being the highest system in regard to these values, the fact of the matter is that we have internal difficulties which occasionally break out and demonstrate our own weaknesses and our own conflicts, and therefore threaten these myths. . . . In the past, arguments have been offered that we would have to submit ourselves to the judgment of others who are our enemies. . . . I think in the past the fear has been, first, that our myths would be

undermined, and second, that we really would find ourselves being put in the docket in a number of instances in regard to human rights situations in our country—for example, the situation of native Americans, or of blacks, Chicanos, women, and so on.[23]

This concern that the United States does not live up to the values it espouses or that it is fearful of giving others the right to examine us, as we are given to examining them, would have the same effect on foreign policy as Dwain Epps's statement. Such awareness as Dr. Wipfler is suggesting would infuse U.S. policy with humility and thus probably add an element of prudence, understood as restraint, to U.S. human rights policy.

One problem of course is that, whenever truth is expressed by humans and human institutions, it is inevitably compromised by sinfulness, and frequently an awareness of that is debilitating or at least inhibits the expression of that truth. Put more concretely, how can U.S. human rights policy be vigorously promoted if the United States doubts its ability to approximate the human rights standards it is rhetorically upholding?

The problem raised by Dr. Wipfler—that the United States did not want its human rights practices examined in the international arena— echoed an historical U.S. concern. In an *amicus* brief filed by the American Association for the United Nations in *Shelley v. Kraemer* (1948), it was claimed that Articles 55 and 56 of the United Nations Charter had transformed human rights from a domestic to an international matter. This argument led Sen. John Bricker (R. Ohio) to introduce an amendment to limit U.S. participation in UN human rights covenants.[24] While the amendment did not pass, it, nevertheless, represented a deep-seated concern for many in the United States. Consequently, not only was the United States to be prudent in how it promoted human rights because of its own limitations in that area but also because the United States has been reluctant to make itself open to international scrutiny in the area. (Prudence in this context, of course, means restraint resulting not only from fear but also from moral sensitivity.)

According to Dr. Wipfler the United States, standing in humility before the facts of American experience, ought to ratify the human rights covenants. In that same series of statements representatives for the Lutheran Council in the U.S.A., the Association of Evangelical Lutheran Churches, the American Lutheran Church, and the Lutheran Church in

America argued that, though some may see international covenants and conventions as a mere "paper barrier," there is real value in public solemn enunciation of legal norms "regardless of the power of groups or nations to violate them."[25]

With regard to the specific issue of support for the Helsinki Accord, Bishop William F. Creighton of the Episcopal Diocese of Washington sent a letter to Rep. Dante Fascell endorsing the establishment of the Commission on Security and Cooperation in Europe. In that letter Bishop Creighton wrote, "It is of importance to the churches that the provisions of the Helsinki Agreement be monitored, especially, of course, from the point of view of religious freedom."[26] In addition to this letter, a resolution from the "Eighty-first Annual Convention of the Diocese of Washington, Episcopal of January 3031, 1976" was included in the record of the testimony. This resolution was in support of the proposed legislation to establish a commission to monitor compliance with the provisions of the Helsinki Final Act, "especially those relating to cooperation in humanitarian affairs. . . ."[27]

The approach to human rights advocacy, we have seen, warns against self-righteousness, questions U.S. motives for not participating fully in existing human rights agreements, and encourages the United States to promote human rights by withdrawing support from repressive governments and monitoring compliance with the Helsinki Final Act's human rights provisions. Yet the weight of evidence suggests a less rigorous stand vis-à-vis human rights abuses in the Soviet Union and Eastern Europe in comparison with other issues. In summary three reasons are apparent why the churches were reluctant to be too critical of Soviet human rights abuses: (1) there was a prudential reluctance to heat up the Cold War; (2) there was a realization, especially at the WCC, that criticism of the Soviet Union might endanger the participants from that society as well as jeopardize the interchurch relations between WCC communions and the Eastern European churches; and (3) there was a theological inhibition against condemning others for human rights violations when our own record was far from perfect. The possible fourth reason, NCCC and WCC ideological bias toward the left, seems a more tenuous explanation in light of the NCCC's earlier hostility toward Soviet communism.[28] This fourth explanation seems less likely as well because of continued documentation of human rights abuses and oppression in

Eastern Europe (e.g., the Soviet intervention in the "Prague Spring" in 1968, and Soviet support of martial law in Poland in 1981). The death of ideological fervor in the Soviet Union, long before the dissolution of the country itself, meant the Soviet Union did not have the same utopian attraction for leftists worldwide that it had had during the early years following the Russian Revolution of 1917.

How Effective Were the Churches?

Determining the effectiveness of any group on public policy is extremely difficult. As David Forsythe writes:

> Understanding the influence exerted by groups on public policy is one of the "most critical and difficult" issues of political analysis. The difficulty of factoring out of multiple causations the single supposedly independent role of groups is widely recognized.[29]

Rarely is it possible to identify one cause as being dominant in a policymaker's decision, and rarely does any one group convert any official. Because of his personal support for human rights and the greater accessibility of Protestant groups to him than his predecessors, one might conclude that President Carter would have been more susceptible to influence, but even with President Carter it is clear that numerous factors influenced his policymaking.

As described in the last chapter, U.S. public opinion on the Helsinki Accord shifted. Kissinger's position modified. A Helsinki Commission was set up by Congress. Helsinki Watch groups were established. And during the time frame under discussion Jimmy Carter, a candidate with a personal commitment to human rights, became president. All this is to suggest that within American society, even apart from the urgings of mainline Protestant churches, there were influences at work to cause foreign policy toward Europe to reflect more concern for human rights.

Even so, individuals associated with the NCCC have taken some credit for U.S. human rights policy in general, if not with specific reference to the CSCE, as follows:

Several nonprofit staffers argued that it had been their groups which had "defined the background" against which [Congressman Donald] Fraser and later Carter had acted. They believed their focus on the moral, human, and human rights issues in Vietnam and in American foreign policy in general had helped create a climate of opinion in which certain officials had then taken specific initiatives. For example, individuals associated with the National Council of Churches argued that it was their concern with torture in Brazil and American funding for foreign police training which, with the support of Senators Church, Abourezk, and others, had really started the renewed U.S. concern for human rights between 1969 and 1971.[30]

Thus apart from specific suggestions made in testimony, the churches' human rights advocacy can make a difference even if only in the eyes of the advocates.

In regard to the specific issues being addressed by the churches outlined above, it can be said that the outcomes were by and large those advocated by the churches. There are now, for example, human rights statements on each country receiving U.S. foreign aid (so that a nation violating human rights can be threatened with a cutoff of aid); the human rights covenants were approved by the Senate; a Helsinki Commission was established; and human rights were monitored in the countries signatory to the Helsinki Final Act. Thus a high correlation can be found even if no cause and effect can be established.

At this point a word of caution should be raised about the question of effectiveness and the somewhat overlooked assumption about for whom the churches speak. The one temptation for church leaders to fall into is that which says official positions of denominations are clearly speaking for God. The temptation is to believe that church pronouncements and the actions they are meant to produce are truly prophetic and are consistent with the mind of Christ. Dr. Paul Ramsey, the late professor of religion at Princeton University, warned of too specific political pronouncements that do not reflect prudent political judgment and that come from church bodies whose Christian perspective does not add anything to the political debate.[31] The choice need not be between saying nothing about the moral context and consequences of policy and saying too much, as Dr. Ramsey himself concedes, but rather saying, with appropriate humility, the proper thing. It is with that understanding that the chapter now turns to the nature of Christian realism.

The Churches' Witness and Christian Realism

In attempting to influence foreign policy in the United States the mainline Protestant churches are aware of two demands. First, they are aware of the need to speak in a way that will be faithful to their own theological self-understanding. Second, they are aware of the need to communicate in a language that will enlist support for their positions, recognizing that the U.S. society is pluralistic both religiously and philosophically. (The secular nature of U.S. society can breed outright hostility toward anyone taking a position based on religious beliefs.) Reconciling these two demands is not always easy. In the context of politicians used to diverse constituencies, outright hostility is unlikely even if religious convictions referred to by church leaders in testimony may not be shared by the politicians.

It is in this context that the language of Christian realism can be helpful. Reinhold Niebuhr, as the foremost proponent of Christian realism, defined that language both for the religious community and for politicians. As professor of Christian social ethics at Union Theological Seminary, he spoke about the political world to religionists. As an activist and adviser to George F. Kennan's Policy Planning Staff of the State Department, he spoke of the public policy issues as he saw them in light of his theological understanding.

In Niebuhr's Christian realism, the "realism" refers to his view that human nature displays both self-regarding and other-regarding tendencies. Thus Niebuhr writes:

> In analysing the limits of reason in morality it is important to begin by recognizing that the force of egoistic impulse is much more powerful than any but the most astute psychological analysts and the most rigorous devotees of introspection realise. If it is defeated on a lower or more obvious level, it will express itself in more subtle forms. If it is defeated by social impulse it insinuates itself into the social impulse, so that a man's devotion to his community always means the expression of a transferred egoism as well as altruism. Reason may check egoism in

order to fit it harmoniously into a total body of social impulse. But the same force of reason is bound to justify the egoism of the individual as a legitimate element in the total body of vital capacities, which society seeks to harmonise.[32]

Niebuhr argues as well that groups magnify the self-regarding tendencies in individuals. He writes:

In every human group there is less reason to guide and to check impulse, less capacity for self-transcendence, less ability to comprehend the needs of others and therefore more unrestrained egoism than the individuals, who compose the group, reveal in their personal relationships. The inferiority of the morality of groups to that of individuals is due in part to the difficulty of establishing a rational social force which is powerful enough to cope with the natural impulses by which society achieves its cohesion; but in part it is merely the revelation of a collective egoism, compounded of the egoistic impulses of individuals, which achieve a more vivid expression and a more cumulative effect when they are united in a common impulse than when they express themselves separately and discreetly.[33]

According to Niebuhr's Christian realism relations among groups reflect the relative power of the groups. Thus he writes:

It may be possible, though it is never easy, to establish just relations between individuals within a group purely by moral and rational suasion and accommodation. In inter-group relations this is practically an impossibility. The relations between groups must therefore always be predominantly political rather than ethical, that is, they will be determined by the proportion of power which each group possesses at least as much as by any rational and moral appraisal of the comparative needs and claims of each group. The coercive factors, in distinction to the more purely moral and rational factors, in political relations can never be sharply differentiated and defined.[34]

This analysis leads Niebuhr to view the relevant moral norm for ordering society as justice informed by love, not simply as love itself. Justice stands in dialectical relationship to love in that justice is the approximation of love in the life of society, but justice is always judged by the ideal of love. Thus Niebuhr writes:

> All structures of justice do indeed presuppose the sinfulness of man, and are all partly systems of restraint which prevent the conflict of wills and interests from resulting in a consistent anarchy. But they are also all mechanisms by which men fulfill their obligations to their fellow men, beyond the possibilities offered in direct and personal relationships. The Kingdom of God and the demands of perfect love are therefore relevant to every political system and impinge upon every social situation in which the self seeks to come to terms with the claims of other life. . . . Translated into these terms the Christian conception of the relation of historical justice to the love of the Kingdom of God is a dialectical one. Love is both the fulfillment and the negation of all achievements of justice in history. Or expressed from the opposite standpoint, the achievements of justice in history may rise in indeterminate degrees to find their fulfillment in a more perfect love and brotherhood; but each new level of fulfillment also contains elements which stand in contradiction to perfect love. There are therefore obligations to realize justice in indeterminate degrees; but none of the realizations can assure the serenity of perfect fulfillment.[35]

In foreign policy this awareness of power manifests itself in Niebuhr's concern for the national interest. Even though he recognizes the importance of national interest, Niebuhr argues that it should not be defined too narrowly. Thus he writes:

> The selfishness of nations is proverbial. It was a dictum of George Washington that nations were not to be trusted beyond their own interest. . . . What is the basis and reason for the selfishness of nations? If we begin with what is least important or least distinctive of national attitudes, it must be noted that nations do not have direct contact with other national communities, with which they must form some kind of international community. They know the problems of other peoples only indirectly and at second hand. Since both sympathy and justice depend to a large degree upon the perception of need, which makes sympathy flow, and upon the understanding of competing interests, which must be resolved, it is obvious that human communities have greater difficulty than individuals in achieving ethical relationships. . . .

. Since their (nations') ultimate interests are always protected best, by
at least a measure of fairness toward their neighbors, the desire to gain
an immediate selfish advantage always imperils their ultimate interests.
If they recognise this fact, they usually recognise it too late.[36]

Thus, as will be seen in subsequent chapters, Niebuhr's understanding of
the national interest is somewhat different from that of other realists. It
may well be the Christian element in his Christian realism that makes this
difference. Thus Larry Rasmussen, Reinhold Niebuhr Professor of Social
Ethics at Union Theological Seminary, writes:

The qualifier "Christian" injects the critical theological element, and
leads directly to the structure of Niebuhr's thought as one of
idealism/realism. Niebuhr characteristically moved between the polar
elements of certain theologically crucial pairs. Both terms of each pair
were equally real for him: the ideal and the real, the absolute and the
contingent, the infinite and the finite, the eternal Kingdom of God and
the flux of history. "Christian" in "Christian realism" places realism in
a theological context which includes all these elements.[37]

It is in his ability to draw on both polar elements that Niebuhr is able to
avoid utopianism on the one hand or cynicism on the other. In evaluating
the theological positions of mainline Protestant churches, one should keep
in mind these polar elements in order to see if their pronouncements are as
nuanced and helpful in guiding decision-makers.

It should be remembered here that what Niebuhr was seeking in his
movement between these polar elements is a Christian ethic that accepts
human sinfulness as a given. His ethic is one of responsibility, not one of
moral purity. He is attempting to make moral decisions in a fallen world,
not in the best possible world imaginable. Thus in dispute with his brother
over the proper response to the Sino-Japanese conflict of the early 1930s,
Niebuhr writes:

I realize quite well that my brother's position both in its ethical
perfectionism and in its apocalyptic note is closer to the gospel than
mine. In confessing that, I am forced to admit that I am unable to
construct an adequate social ethic out of a pure love ethic. I cannot
abandon the pure love ideal because anything which falls short of it is

less than ideal. But I cannot use it fully if I want to assume a responsible attitude toward the problems of society. Religious perfectionism drives either to asceticism or apocalypticism. In the one case the problem of society is given up entirely; in the other individual perfection is regarded as the force which will release the redemptive powers of God for society. I think the second alternative is better than the first, and that both have elements which must be retained for any adequate social ethic, lest it become lost in the relativities of expediency. But as long as the world of man remains a place where nature and God, the real and the ideal, meet, human progress will depend upon the judicious use of the forces of nature in the service of the ideal.[38]

The Protestant churches under consideration tend to avoid a pietistic noninvolvement with politics on the one hand or theologies given to uncritical endorsement of nationalism on the other. These churches have been able to draw on Social Gospel theology for their activism. The thrust of the Social Gospel can be seen in the title of a book by Walter Rauschenbusch, a leader of the movement, *Christianizing the Social Order*. Reinhold Niebuhr criticized the Social Gospel movement for its "soft utopianism" and its exaggerated faith in human ability to overcome sin and social ills. For the purposes of international relations Niebuhr's concern over power and competing interests tended to show the weakness of Social Gospel thought.

In evaluating the political positions advocated by mainline Protestant churches, one should keep in mind the category of realism and the concepts of national interest and power related to it. Do the churches' statements enhance or detract from U.S. power? Or do the statements merely assume U.S. power and appear to be otherwise indifferent to the implications of their positions toward U.S. power in the world? Do the positions advocated by the churches reveal a particular perspective on what is the U.S. national interest? What might be an enlightened national interest in keeping with Christian realism?

In both the testimony of Dr. Randall and Dr. Wipfler the power of the United States is assumed. The point of both statements was not to enhance the power of the nation. It could be argued that it is not the role of religious leaders to make any nation more powerful. Nevertheless, it would seem wise for any organization attempting to influence U.S. foreign policy to couch its position in a way that would enhance that organization's credibility. This is especially true if an organization is known to have a history of criticism of U.S. foreign policy. In his testimony Dr. Wipfler notes how the NCCC has been critical of U.S. human rights policy when he states:

> we (the NCCC) have moved from a position of challenge to disappointment and finally to criticism because of what we feel is the abdication of the United States from a position of leadership in international efforts to establish an adequate framework to guarantee the protection of human rights.[39]

In her testimony (delivered three years before Dr. Wipfler's) Dr. Randall had used terms that could resonate with politicians responsible for the foreign policy and national security of the United States. Her statement, "There is a need for a new definition of national interest"[40] could have come directly from Reinhold Niebuhr. Although concern for the national interest is not synonymous with concern for power, at least it is a term that expresses a sensitivity for policymakers because they are aware of their responsibility for the national interest.

In her concern for "a new definition of national interest" Dr. Randall uses the terminology of political realism[41] and does so in a way consistent with Christian realism. The reason national interest needs a "new definition," according to Dr. Randall's testimony, is to take into account the interdependence of modern international society. Dr. Randall quotes from a National Council of Churches resolution that "our neighbor's growth is part of our growth. We seek their wellbeing in partnership for peace, realizing that we are mutually dependent for security."[42] This rather expansive view of the national interest was a view Niebuhr alluded to as early as 1932 in *Moral Man and Immoral Society* when he wrote:

> Perhaps the best that can be expected of nations is that they should justify their hypocrisies by a slight measure of international achievement, and learn how to do justice to wider interests than their own, while they pursue their own.[43]

The Christian realist perspective shares with political realism generally the need for the policymaker to set policy in terms of the national interest. Niebuhr believes that the wise political leader will understand the importance of seeing one's own national interest as broadly encompassing the national interest of other countries. For example, the U.S. security interests, and therefore national interest, are enhanced by recognizing the legitimate security interests of the Soviet Union. Put another way the United States will be more secure if the Soviet Union is more secure, up to a point.

What it means to have a broadened or enlightened concept of national interest may not always be evident. In his 1979 testimony Dr. Wipfler refers to the NCCC judgment of 1968:

> The United States has defeated its true national interest by hoarding sovereignty in respect to reservations upon employment of the International Court of Justice and failure to ratify conventions on human rights.[44]

It is not clear whether "hoarding sovereignty" serves "true national interest" or not. There seems to be an element of liberal idealism, or utopianism, operating because ratification of human rights agreements can serve to undermine sovereignty, which is the defining characteristic of the state. That is to say, it may be in the best interest of humanity to restrict national sovereignty but not in the state's interest as a nation.

In his presentation Dr. Wipfler also makes the important connection between NCCC support for international human rights covenants and U.S. values and the principles embodied in the U.S. Constitution.[45] In making this connection he legitimates both U.S. values and the Constitution, from the perspective of mainline Protestant Christians, and the mainline Protestant churches, from the perspective of political leadership. This connection fosters the national myth that Wipfler refers to earlier both in his testimony and above in this chapter.

Reinhold Niebuhr knew that this mythmaking process is both natural and important to the maintenance of the state. He writes:

> Every class and nation defends itself and justifies its interests by a social myth. The myth also is used to detract from the moral prestige of

adversaries. Social myths are constructed by imaginative elaborations of actual history. They are hardly ever made out of whole cloth. They arise because reason is more ambiguous in relation to the individual or social self than some rationalists assume. Reason is never the sole master of the acquisitive and anxious self. It is always part master and part servant of that self, particularly the collective self of the nation.[46]

Yet as important as the social myth is in defining and defending the United States, to say nothing of its role in fighting the Cold War, there was a reluctance on the part of mainline Protestant churches to promote the American social myth of U.S. righteousness too vigorously. The reluctance of the NCCC and its constituent members to give too much rhetorical support to this social myth reflects another concern of Christian realism as well, the tendency of a nation to overstate its own virtue. Niebuhr clearly warns about this tendency when he writes:

> Perhaps the most significant moral characteristic of a nation is its hypocrisy. We have noted that self-deception and hypocrisy is an unvarying element in the moral life of all human beings. . . . Naturally this defect in individuals becomes more apparent in the less moral life of nations. Yet it might be supposed that nations, of whom so much less is expected, would not be under the necessity of making moral pretensions for their actions. There was probably a time when they were under no such necessity. Their hypocrisy is both a tribute to the growing rationality of man and a proof of the ease with which rational demands may be circumvented.[47]

The American Baptist Churches, a member communion of the NCCC, adopted a "Policy Statement on Human Rights" in December 1976 that expressed the tension between the social myth and the concern with national pride. After recounting the Baptists' historical concern for religious liberty, the policy statement states:

> The United States carries a particular responsibility in human rights because of its basic historical commitment to freedom and because of the power it wields in the world and the influence it has on other countries. It is important, therefore, in view of wide scale violation of human rights in our world today, even in our own nation, that

American Baptists address a comprehensive statement of concerns to ourselves, our nation and other nations.[48]

The acknowledgment of the United States' historical commitment to freedom and the acknowledgment of the existence of human rights violations in the United States effectively balances the social myth with Christian humility. In a similar way the United Church of Christ in "The Church Pronouncement on Human Rights" states:

> As Christians in the United States we affirm our history of struggle for democratic and civil rights of the individual. We may not give up the gains which have been made in this history or the valid emphasis on the rights of the individual and the community over against the state. Our task is to use this democratic tradition to spread civil and individual rights into the economic, cultural and natural dimensions. We commit ourselves to the best in our tradition. As Christians we also confess our own failures to achieve a society which fully protects the human rights of all our citizens.[49]

This statement shows even more restraint than that of the American Baptists in referring to human rights in U.S. history. The UCC document goes even further by stating:

> [It] Commends to the churches, church-related agencies, associations, conferences and national agencies of the United Church of Christ, the study and consideration of the Petition of Human Rights Violations in the United States to the United Nations Commission on Human Rights and Sub-Commission on Prevention of Discrimination and Protection of Minorities, submitted by the Commission for Racial Justice of the UCC and others.[50]

The use of the word "struggle" in the UCC document suggests even less accomplishment of the social myth than the American Baptist policy statement. The direct reference to the possibility of petitioning the United Nations over human rights abuses makes it even more difficult to harbor illusions about the social myth that the United States is the great promoter of human rights.

Two points should be made about both the "American Baptist Policy Statement on Human Rights" and the "United Church Pronouncement on Human Rights." First, these documents are primarily internal to the denominations themselves and are only indirectly used in influencing makers of U.S. foreign policy. Second, since they are internal documents, they have their greatest impact on the churches within the denominations.

The subtlety of these documents might make it more difficult for human rights activists to urge an aggressive U.S. human rights policy in the CSCE than would statements more blindly accepting of the social myth. (Of course blind acceptance of the social myth would be both morally wrong and historically inaccurate.) Reinhold Niebuhr seems to support this contention when he writes, "Contending factions in a social struggle require morale; and morale is created by the right dogmas, symbols and emotionally potent oversimplifications."[51] Neither of these documents seems to suggest "emotionally potent oversimplifications." In these instances at least there is no pointed expression of the moral superiority of liberal democracy over Communist societies.

It should not be surprising that the evidence suggests an affinity between policy pronouncements and public policy advocacy, on the one hand, and the Christian realism of Reinhold Niebuhr, on the other. As Max Stackhouse has written:

> The directions charted by the Social Gospel and by "Christian Realism," under Niebuhr's leadership, were not to remain solely a conviction of these two. They were taken up by the Federal Council of Churches. . . .[52]

The Federal Council of Churches was the predecessor of the National Council of Churches of Christ. As will be seen in later chapters the Social Gospel and the Christian realist perspectives could pull in different directions.

Summary

The story of the churches' involvement in influencing U.S. human rights policy toward the Final Act as well as the subsequent CSCE process is mixed. On the one hand, there is little evidence of much direct involvement of mainline Protestant churches either with Congress or with the president in attempting to influence U.S. policy on human rights with regard to Helsinki. On the other, there is concern via the World Council of Churches and the National Council of Churches that Christian churches examine how human rights could be promoted in accordance with the Helsinki Final Act. Even so the WCC and NCCC program specific to Helsinki did not get underway until 1980.

A more fruitful way of looking at the possible influence of the mainline Protestant churches on human rights is to see that they were active in attempting to promote a U.S. human rights policy in the context of other regions of the world. The arguments made in favor of human rights, it has been argued, had a spillover effect on U.S. human rights policy generally.

In the statements before the relevant congressional committees that were examined, it was found that policies the groups had advocated were frequently adopted. The State Department prepares country reports on human rights as a precondition for foreign aid. The international human rights treaties were adopted. Most important for the purposes of this chapter, in the follow-up conferences on the Helsinki Final Act, the United States took an active role in seeking compliance with the human rights provisions. This scorecard is not meant to establish a cause and effect relationship, but it is meant to suggest the possibility of influence for the churches.

David Forsythe has written:

> The resources of lobbyists include first and foremost the quality of the information they seek to impart; second, the legitimacy of the lobby within the context of societal values; and then in no particular order money, membership, organization, and leadership.[53]

The churches, when they act as lobbying organizations, can evaluate the likelihood that they will be effective by the above criteria. The concerns expressed in Christian realism for humility, for an understanding of the facts of the case (including appeal to the concept of national interest), and of the necessity of foreign policy to use the national myth, could all have enhanced the effectiveness of church testimony. As the above analysis makes clear the churches positions were consistent with Christian realism.

The material from the NCCC and various Protestant churches provide high quality information, and by supporting our national myth seem to give the churches legitimacy within the context of societal values.

The subtlety of the statements analyzed suggest an awareness of the need for both humility and prudence in the realm of U.S. human rights policy. The prudential nature is somewhat more difficult to discern from the statements because the statements tended to involve areas of the world less likely to lead to superpower confrontation. Most of the statements analyzed tended to talk of human rights in relation to U.S. client states rather than to raise an issue of superpower discourse. Yet the analysis shows clearly the concern for humility in U.S. human rights policy, a characteristic emphasis of Christian realism.

Another aspect of how the mainline Protestant churches can have an impact on U.S. human rights policy is how those churches influence the American culture generally. The shift from Gerald Ford to Jimmy Carter was significant (as comments by Soviet dissident Natan Shransky and Cyrus Vance will show). Apart from the influence President Carter said Reinhold Niebuhr had on him, a matter to be explored in the following chapter, what other Protestant influences may have made an impact on the culture and thus on U.S. human rights policy? How does a religious group articulate its position in a pluralistic society? It is to that question that the discussion turns in the next chapter.

Notes

1. A review of the *Public Papers of the Presidents* from 1969 through 1977 shows no meetings between the presidents and the National Council of Churches.

2. David P. Forsythe, *Human Rights and World Politics*, 2d ed. (Lincoln: University of Nebraska Press, 1989), 132.

3. Mr. Jim Hamilton, director of the National Council of Churches Washington Office, telephone interview by author, 16 September 1996. The nature of this meeting was confirmed in a telephone interview with Dr. Claire Randall of 1 November 1996. Dr. Randall's perception of President Carter's statement was that the president was really showing his support of human rights by this statement. The concern over the most segregated hour in America was, according to Dr. Randall, a well-practiced refrain from the days of the

civil rights struggle. Dr. Randall thus saw the president's remarks less as a scolding than did Mr. Hamilton.

4. "Background Memorandum for President Carter Regarding Concerns which Officers and Leaders of the National Council of Churches Want to Discuss with Him at Their Meeting, February 24, 1978," in the files of the NCC Washington Office.

5. Forsythe, *Human Rights and World Politics*, 127-159.

6. Forsythe, *Human Rights and World Politics*, 149.

7. Claire Randall, Testimony Before the Senate Foreign Relations Committee, January 21, 1976, 9, from the files of the Washington Office of the National Council of Churches of Christ in the U.S.A.

8. Randall, Testimony before the Senate Foreign Relations Committee, 14.

9. Lowell W. Livezey, *Nongovernmental Organizations and the Ideas of Human Rights*, Publication of The Center for International Studies, World Order Studies Program Occasional Paper, no. 15 (Princeton, N.J.: Princeton University Press, 1988), 70.

10. The letter is Appendix I, in Max L. Stackhouse, *Creeds, Society, and Human Rights: A Study in Three Cultures* (Grand Rapids, Mich.: William B. Eerdmans Publishing Company, 1984), 284-85.

11. Livezey, *Nongovernmental Organizations*, 66.

12. Congress, Senate, Committee on Foreign Relations, *International Human Rights Treaties: Hearings before the Committee on Foreign Relations*, 96th Cong., 1st sess., 14, 15, 16, 19 November 1979, 352.

13. Dr. Charles E. Cobb, "Report to Inter-unit Committee on International Concerns on the Working Committee of the Churches' Human Rights Programme for the Implementation of the Helsinki Final Act" January 13 1984, from the files of the Washington Office of the National Council of Churches of Christ in the U.S.A., 2.

14. Leary, "The Implementation of the Human Rights Provisions," 159.

15. Robert Traer, *Faith in Human Rights: Support in Religious Traditions for a Global Struggle* (Washington, D.C.: Georgetown University Press, 1991), 22.

16. Leary, "The Implementation of the Human Rights Provisions," 134-35.

17. Leary, "The Implementation of the Human Rights Provisions," 135-37.

18. Max Stackhouse, "Public Theology, Human Rights and Missions," in *Human Rights and the Global Mission of the Church*, by the Boston Theological Institute (Cambridge, Mass.: Boston Theological Institute, 1985), 16.

19. Cobb, "Report to Inter-unit Committee on International Concerns," 1.

20. Leary, "The Implementation of the Human Rights Provisions," 137-38.

21. David M. Paton, ed., *Breaking Barriers Nairobi 1975: The Official Report of the Fifth Assembly of the World Council of Churches, Nairobi, 23 November 10 December, 1975* (Grand Rapids, Mich.: William B. Eerdmans Publishing Company, 1976), 30, 171-72.

22. Letter from Dwain C. Epps to Congresswoman Millicent Fenwick dated 1 June 1976, in the files of the Washington Office of the National Council of Churches of Christ.

23. Congress, Senate, Committee on Foreign Relations, *International Human Rights Treaties*, 96th Cong., 1st sess., 19 November 1979, 415-16.

24. Jo Renee Formicola, "The American Catholic Church and Its Role in the Formulation of United States Human Rights Foreign Policy 1945-1978" (Ph.D. diss., Drew University, 1981), 141.

25. Congress, Senate, *Human Rights Treaties*, 407-9.

26. Congress, House of Representatives, Committee on International Relations, *Conference on Security and Cooperation in Europe: Part II, Hearings before the Subcommittee on International Political and Military Affairs of the Committee on International Relations.* 94th Cong., 4 May 1976, 107.

27. House, *Conference on Security and Cooperation in Europe.*

28. For early official NCC statements opposing communism see Lloyd Billingsley's *From Mainline to Sideline: The Social Witness of the National Council of Churches* (Washington, D.C.: Ethics and Public Policy Center, 1990).

29. Forsythe, *Human Rights and World Politics*, 140.

30. Forsythe, *Human Rights and World Politics*, 142.

31. Paul Ramsey, *Who Speaks for the Church?: A Critique of the 1966 Geneva Conference on Church and Society* (N.Y.: Abingdon Press, 1967), 13.

32. Reinhold Niebuhr, *Moral Man and Immoral Society: A Study in Ethics and Politics* (N.Y.: Charles Scribner's Sons, 1960), 40-41.

33. 33 Niebuhr, *Moral Man*, xixii.

34. Niebuhr, *Moral Man*, xxiixxiii.

35. Reinhold Niebuhr, *The Nature and Destiny of Man* Vol. 2, *Human Nature* (N.Y.: Charles Scribner's Sons, 1943), 192, 246.

36. Niebuhr, *Moral Man*, 84-86.

37. Larry Rasmussen, ed., "Reinhold Niebuhr: Theologian of Public Life," in *The Making of Modern Theology*, gen. ed. John de Gruchy, from the introduction by Larry Rasmussen (London: Collins, 1988) 20-21.

38. Reinhold Niebuhr, "Must We Do Nothing?" in *The Christian Century Reader: Representative Articles, Editorials, and Poems Selected from More*

than Fifty Years of the Christian Century, ed. Harold E. Fey and Margaret Frakes (N.Y.: Association Press, 1962), 226-27.

39. Wipfler, *International Human Rights Treaties*, 353.

40. Randall, Testimony, 21 January 1976, 3.

41. Morgenthau and Thompson, *Politics among Nations*, 10-11.

42. Randall, Testimony, 21 January 1976, 3.

43. Niebuhr, *Moral Man*, 108.

44. Wipfler, *International Human Rights Treaties*, 353.

45. Wipfler, *International Human Rights Treaties*, 354.

46. Reinhold Niebuhr, "The Social Myths in the Cold War," *Journal of International Affairs* (1967), reprinted in *Faith and Politics: A Commentary on Religious, Social and Political Thought in a Technological Age*, ed. Ronald H. Stone (N.Y.: George Braziller, 1968), 223.

47. Niebuhr, *Moral Man*, 95.

48. American Baptist, "Policy Statement on Human Rights," adopted December 1976, 1.

49. Stackhouse, *Creeds, Society, and Human Rights*, 297.

50. Stackhouse, *Creeds, Society, and Human Rights.*, 299.

51. Niebuhr, *Moral Man*, xv.

52. Stackhouse, *Creeds, Society, and Human Rights*, 121.

53. Forsythe, *Human Rights and World Politics*, 132.

Chapter 4

The Churches' Influence in a Pluralistic Context

The last chapter dealt with how Protestant churches in the United States sought to influence directly U.S. human rights policy in relation to the CSCE. This chapter focuses on the more indirect ways in which the churches have influenced U.S. culture generally and American attitudes on human rights specifically. In light of the thesis of this study, that Christian realism provides the most adequate ethic for U.S. human rights policy in the CSCE, the strength of Christian realism in articulating ethics in a pluralistic context will be highlighted.

The chapter is divided into three parts. The first part will explore the meaning of human rights. It will reveal not only the philosophical background but also the scriptural foundations for understanding human rights. Both philosophical and biblical material is accessible to society and has played an influential role in forming the society. The second part will discuss the existence of an "American creed" and its relationship to biblical faith. This public philosophy will be shown to enhance the ability of religionists to use some religious language in public discourse. The third part will examine how Christian realism, because of its concerns and language, particularly aids in the understanding of human rights in most pluralistic contexts. Christian realism will be shown to take seriously cultural differences and thereby strengthen its arguments for understanding human rights, even if the scope of rights may be defined more narrowly than by the idealists.

It should be kept in mind that throughout its history the United States has been characterized by religious diversity. Before it was one nation, what was to become the United States was inhabited by people of diverse religious convictions and denominations. The act of establishing the Constitution and Bill of Rights focused attention on how we were to live with our differing beliefs about religion and God. In the years since 1789 the country has become even more pluralistic. The challenge to the Christian church represented by this pluralism is threefold: first, the message of the church must maintain the integrity of its theological convictions; second, to the extent that it wishes to be effective the church must speak its truth in a way that can be apprehended by a significant number of people who may not share its theological understanding or its language; and third, to the extent that the church supports a liberal democratic society it must witness in the public arena in a way that reinforces liberal democracy.

Human Rights: What Are They? Where Do They Come From?

The first question that needs to be addressed is: What are human rights? With so much attention being paid to human rights in the press, in political circles, and in the academy, one might expect there to be a clear definition of the concept. That is not the case. Part of the confusion stems from the use of the term "human rights" to refer to philosophy, political activism, and legal concepts. Another reason for the confusion is that the term has become an all-encompassing symbol for activists promoting a wide variety of claims. Adding to the difficulty of defining human rights is the fact that human rights have both a descriptive and a normative character. That is, human rights can be said to be something one has (their descriptive character) as well as something to which one aspires (their normative character). Thus, as one philosopher put it, though human rights are impossible to ignore, they are hard to define because they are not simply the result of philosophical argument but are the result of experience and history. [1]

In an article comparing and contrasting American legal rights and human rights, legal scholar Louis Henkin writes:

> American rights need no introduction. As every schoolchild can recite our rights are proclaimed in the Declaration of Independence and protected by the Constitution. Americans are aware of their rights, as if in their blood. We live our rights in our lives, daily. Human rights . . . are now spoken of easily in every language, in national politics and international diplomacy, in the learned jargon of professions and academic disciplines. . . . [B]y "human rights" I mean simply those moral-political claims which, by contemporary consensus, every human being has or is deemed to have upon his society and government. These claims are enumerated in contemporary international instruments—in the Universal Declaration of Human Rights, which has been accepted by virtually all governments . . . and in international agreements to which more and more nations are adhering at a steady rate.[2]

This definition of human rights identifies the nature of a human right as a moral-political claim. While the definition states that human beings make the claim, it does not suggest, as this essay will, that the claim stems from the human being's existence as a human being. This claim that simply because one is a human being one has rights is important for making the connection for Christian churches and for an understanding of the connection with the biblical affirmation that all people are created in God's image. It is not meant to suggest that all persons must subscribe to the biblical affirmation or be Christians in order to espouse human rights. The affirmation that rights stem from one's being a human being is meant to do two things: first, it is meant to show how Christian churches might influence American society on the issue of rights; and second, it is meant to underscore the universality of human rights. As will be shown, one of the most difficult problems in promoting human rights is showing their universal character. Finally, it should be kept in mind that Henkin's definition states that the claim is made by the individual on his or her society and government. This last point signifies that while we are writing about human rights in relation to international relations and foreign policy, the claim itself is directed at one government or one society. For example, even though Andre Sakharov may have contacted the CSCE on behalf of someone whose rights, under the Helsinki Accord, may have been violated, the claim was against the Soviet Union—not against the international community or any other signatory to the Accord. Even though human rights may be universal, that is, the same for all individuals wherever they are, they are claims against a specific society or government. Concern with the international legal ramifications of individuals taking their claims to an international forum to force a particular state to comply with human rights agreements goes beyond the scope of this book.

Professor Henkin's description of human rights provides a good starting point for an elaboration of human rights and their sources. By way of additional clarification as to what is meant by human rights, and why it is not always clear what is being discussed, I would quote J.E. Hare, assistant professor of philosophy at Lehigh University, and Carey B. Joynt, Monroe J. Rathbone professor of international relations at Lehigh University, to the effect that:

> The notion of "rights" is probably best seen as parasitic on the notion of justice. A person has a right to what it is just that he be given. . . . There are at least three ways of translating talk about "rights" into talk about correlative obligations. If I suggest that I have a right to a thing, I may mean simply that it is not wrong for me to have it, or that I should not be prevented from trying to get it, or that I should be given it. Any discussion of "human rights" needs to take account of which of these senses is involved.[3]

In light of Henkin's use of the word "claim" and the contentiousness of the struggle to assert rights in Eastern Europe via the CSCE, it should be clear that for this discussion "human rights" is used in the sense of "I should be given it" identified above. While some human rights activists may make claims that might seem to trivialize the concept, the weightiness of the CSCE human rights provisions suggest actions required of governments.

In practical international negotiations, as seen in chapter one, nations may raise the issue of nonintervention in a state's internal affairs. This problem is exacerbated to the extent that human rights can be said not to have a universal character. Maurice Cranston, professor of political science at the London School of Economics, makes the case for the universality of human rights when he writes:

> There is a very ancient Western tradition of belief both in the reality of natural law—a law higher than the edicts of princes—and of the universal rights that this law confers on all rational, sentient beings. Greeks, Stoics, Romans, medieval Christians, and modern rationalists have sustained much the same conception of basic moral rights that every human being possesses simply by virtue of being human. They are not rights that are conferred exclusively on its members by a particular society. They are universal. And they are inherited, so to speak, with men's humanity itself. Their very generality, however, makes it hard for us to discern these rights at all clearly.[4]

Non-Westerners might be quick to point out that Cranston's argument relies on the Western tradition. While this is true, two related points should be advanced. First, as theologians note, all truth when it is revealed takes on a particularity that mingles that truth with the contingent. Second, as the political process referred to by Henkin makes clear, there has at some level of abstraction (and concreteness) been nearly universal acceptance of human rights documents.

Christian ethicist Robin Lovin reinforces the first point on the universality of human rights when he writes:

> We need to ask, first, "How can we best advocate those rights of freedom which have been the keys to our own political experience?" That's not quite the same thing as promoting "internationally recognized human rights," but it makes it clear that most of those recognized rights have come out of the Western democratic tradition. To recognize the particular historical roots of the rights we prize is not to say that they are relevant only to our society. These rights may be historically, distinctively ours, but we have always held them as truths, not as preferences. The philosopher Leo Strauss once remarked that it does not deny the universality of a political idea to note that it originated in ancient Greece, or in France or in the United States, any more than it makes Newton's Laws particularly British to note that they were discovered in 17th century England.[5]

Important for its implications for foreign policy, the American perspective sees rights universally, according to Louis Henkin, when he writes:

> American rights were proclaimed by Americans in 1776 for themselves. Declared by way of justifying independence from British rule—what we would today call "self-determination"—they reflect a political theory applicable to every human being, in relation to every political society, in every age.[6]

The universality of human rights reveals itself in how these rights are regarded in international society as natural.

> Those who built international human rights also saw these rights as "natural," but in a contemporary sense: human rights correspond to the nature of man and of human society, to his *psychology and its sociology*.[7]

Certainly the "nature of man" refers to a nature that is universally shared, but the implication of Henkin's statement here is that at some level human society's sociology is universal, i.e., since it is natural.

The universal quality of human rights hints at the suprapolitical character of those rights. "(H)uman rights are *moral* rights, as opposed to *legal* or *civil* rights—that is, rights that are recognized and protected by the laws of a particular polity or government."[8] As moral rights, human rights get expressed in positive law. As moral-political claims, as Henkin described them, human rights may be expressed in such documents as the Helsinki Final Act. Yet the Final Act falls somewhere between a document merely expressing moral concerns and a legal document. In fact the CSCE process, as a political process, did more than state moral claims, but it did less than express legal claims, even though it is sometimes difficult to tell given the inchoate nature of international law. Human rights are claims whether realized or not.

It is important to keep in mind that there are two dimensions to human rights understood as claims. They are claims *to* something and *against* someone.[9] In defining the "something," Christians have a role to play; and as illustrated in the civil rights movement in the United States, Christians may often be the "someone" against whom the human rights claims are made. In addition human rights are claims that, because they express moral truth, are valid even if they are not realized in practice.[10] In practical terms the institutional nature of the Christian church facilitates perseverance in advocating human rights.

What, then, are human rights? Human rights are universal moral claims that belong equally to all people by virtue of their being human. These claims have a political nature in that they are brought against a society and government.

Having thus defined human rights, let us turn to the question, What are the sources of human rights? In answering the question, we need to remember that it includes a philosophic dimension as well as an historic dimension. That is, in articulating human rights we are dealing with both what has been philosophically argued as well as what has been experientially recognized as human rights.

"Human rights is a twentieth-century name for what has been traditionally known as Natural Rights or . . . the Rights of Man."[11] Thus, as Maurice Cranston's statement shows, "human rights" is a modern term for an idea that goes back at least to the eighteenth century. Yet if we look not for the term but for the concept of human rights or natural rights we find an even longer lineage. The concept of natural rights or the "Rights of Man"

> traces its philosophical lineage to the Scholastic doctrine of natural law, which, in turn, finds its intellectual origins in the thought of Aristotle and the Greek Stoics and in the moral teachings of Judaism and Christianity.[12]

Aristotle sought the best possible constitution in a given set of circumstances rather than some ideal type. Every state, according to Aristotle, seeks some good.

> Every state is a community of some kind, and every community is established with a view to some good; for mankind always act in order to obtain that which they think good. But, if all communities aim at some good, the state or political community, which is the highest of all, and which embraces all the rest, aims at good in a greater degree than any other, and at the highest good.[13]

As we have already noted (and will further explore) Americans closely identify human rights with the "good" at which we aim, and that has significant implications for U.S. foreign policy.

> The Roman lawyer Cicero is important in political thought because he gave to the Stoic doctrine of natural law a statement in which it was universally known throughout western Europe from his own day down to the nineteenth century. From him it passed to the Roman lawyers and not less to the Fathers of the Church.[14]

Even though Cicero's *Republic* had been lost after the twelfth century and was not rediscovered until the nineteenth century, its most significant passages had been excerpted into other peoples' books, including Augustine's, so that his ideas had become matters of common knowledge.[15] In short, (as Sabine deduces from Cicero) a universal law of nature arises both "from the fact of God's providential government of the world and from the rational and social nature of human beings which makes them akin to God."[16] This law is not only in accord with nature but also applies to all men and is unchangeable and eternal. The Enlightenment reclaimed Cicero, and so he made his impact on America.

Another stream that has influenced Americans (and others) in their understanding of human rights is the Bible. Even though the words "human rights" do not appear in the Bible, Max Stackhouse asserts, "The deepest roots of human rights are found in the biblical conception of life."[17] Several broad biblical themes support the notion of human rights. "Decisive for all human rights thinking and action is the notion that there is a pattern of righteousness which can be known by humans in empirical life but which is not the same as empirical life."[18] Another major biblical theme supporting human rights is the notion that all people are created in the image of God (Genesis 1:26). In respect for that image we are both recipients of human rights claims and claimants against other individuals and, by extension, the society and government.

In addition to the two biblical themes mentioned, there are several other areas of scripture that support human rights activities. In seeing God as a ruler who will one day redress all injustices suffered by the disenfranchised (Luke 18:7), we find support for efforts to end oppression. God created humanity, God's creation is good and thus should be treated with appropriate respect. Wisdom literature, especially the book of Proverbs, insists that we treat each other justly regardless of the particular form of government we live under. (Proverbs, since it does not proclaim the gospel or salvation, exemplifies language that can be appropriated universally.) God's action in Jesus Christ reveals the universality of God's grace, and the biblical witness to God's action in history shows God demanding righteousness from all people. This universality is expressed by Paul when he writes, "When Gentiles who do not have the law do by nature what the law requires, they are a law to themselves, even though they do not have the law. They show that what the law requires is written on their hearts. . . " (Romans 2:1415). All these themes point to powerful scriptural evidence supporting a notion of human rights.[19] Thus biblical evidence and Greek philosophy are two sources of support for human rights influencing American society.

In this writer's opinion, those who place greater weight on the biblical influence are closer to the mark, especially in the American experience. This is the case for several reasons. As uneducated as many people are in regard to classical philosophy or Enlightenment thought, they have been clearly educated as to the demands of God written in the Bible. A major theme that is conveyed in both the Old and New Testaments is the dignity of each person. In the words of Stephen Charles Mott, professor of Christian social ethics at Gordon-Conwell Theological Seminary, "It is God who provides human dignity and consequently human rights."[20] Thus, in an historical vein, the Bible has probably been more influential in transmitting the content of human rights for the mass of people than philosophy.

The Bible is an historical document in at least three senses: (1) it is derived from historical experience, even if it is not a history book per se; (2) it is limited by the historic context in which it was written, e.g., it says nothing about nuclear weapons; (3) it speaks to us in our historic context. In each of these three senses the Bible may or may not be authoritative. For example, a contemporary observer of the Exodus might have concluded that while the Jewish people were liberated from Egypt, the liberation was the work of Moses or perhaps the work of a pagan god but not the work of the God attested to in scripture. Another example of how biblical authority might be questioned would be to point out that the Bible says nothing about birth control pills and, therefore, has nothing authoritative to say about how unwanted pregnancies might be prevented. The Bible is authoritative insofar as the truth it reveals resonates within the heart and mind of the reader (or listener). Christian churches, built around the authoritative Bible, promote human rights as a means of honoring the God whose grace gives humanity its dignity. (It should be added that even among Christians, who read the same Bible and hold that scripture is authoritative, there is not necessarily consensus on what God through the Bible is commanding them to do.)

The Bible is authoritative as a basis for human rights for this writer on three grounds. First, the Bible reveals the God from whose grace human dignity is derived. Human history shows that human beings in and of themselves are too sinful and finite to be the basis for the dignity expressed by human rights. Second, the Bible illuminates the substance of human rights via the moral ideals expressed in scripture. One example of the moral ideal was the institution of the Jubilee Year (Luke 4:19, Isaiah 61:2), designed to systemically address poverty. While there was no actual institution of the year when debts were forgiven, such an event would have had the effect of helping the poor get out of debt. Third, the Bible upholds a moral standard that would continue to critique as well as energize people's commitment to human rights. That standard is known as *agape,* or the sacrificial love of God seen most clearly in the crucifixion of Jesus Christ. It is illustrated in love for the other person, whether that person is the outsider or the alien, because as a child of God he or she is our brother or sister.[21]

Of course, as they participate in the public square, the churches cannot rely on all the members of a pluralistic society to accept the Bible as authoritative. If the churches are to be effective in persuading members of the wider society to support their public policy positions, the churches must make their cases with "publicly accessible reasons." The idea of human dignity and the concept of human rights may be so widely accepted that referring to the source of that dignity and those rights (i.e., for Christians, God) may be unnecessary. Churches may find that for many issues justification for particular policies may need no argument apart from the practical one, namely, does the policy suggested most effectively achieve the end sought? Concern over how churches argue their cases for particular policy positions in a democratic, pluralistic society will be explored more fully later in the chapter.

It should be noted that the concept of human rights is a modern day articulation of natural rights and natural law. Natural law could be understood through right reason. Even though the Protestant Reformers were highly critical of reason, realizing how sin distorts our reasoning, they nevertheless affirmed the importance of natural law.[22]

It was Saint Thomas Aquinas (1225?-1274) who, more than any of the other Scholastics, advanced the ideal of natural law:

> Now among all others, the rational creature is subject to Divine providence in the most excellent way, insofar as it partakes of a share of providence, by being provident both for itself and for others. Wherefore it has a share of the Eternal Reason, whereby it has a natural inclination to its proper act and end: and this participation of the eternal law in the rational creature is called the natural law.[23]

The elaboration of the Thomistic view of natural law aided the development of the ecclesiastical unity of civilization.[24] Troeltsch's "ecclesiastical unity of civilization" may look to some as an attractive feature of a past era, but in practice as well as modern theory the world encourages pluralism that undermines such apparent unity.[25]

Even though Reinhold Niebuhr expressed concerns about the rationality inherent in Thomas's view of natural law, Niebuhr did find principles of natural law he felt more consistent with the New Testament. He writes:

> The principles of "natural law" by which justice is defined are, in fact, not so much fixed standards of reason as they are rational efforts to apply the moral obligation, implied in the love commandment, to the complexities of life and the fact of sin, that is, to the situation created by the inclination of men to take advantage of each other. The most universal norms are also significantly the most negative, such as the prohibition of theft and murder. They define our obligation to the neighbor in such minimal terms that they have achieved almost universal acceptance in the conscience of humanity.[26]

Law is the expression of moral obligation in context. The claim law makes against a person inheres not in law as law but law as expressive of a known moral obligation. "All genuine obedience to law is derived from the grace of love, which is more than law."[27] The significance of this understanding for Niebuhr related to human rights and CSCE will be explored more fully in the last chapter. For now it should be noted that in American history, especially early history, Protestant understandings of natural law probably played a more formative role in America's understanding of human rights than Roman Catholic understandings.

It should be kept in mind that natural law is not synonymous with positive law. Positive law, at its best, is the concrete expression of natural law. Niebuhr is making the point from Christian sources that Cicero and the Stoics make from pagan sources, i.e., that natural law is more than a mere expression of convention. Niebuhr is less inclined than the Stoics to ascribe a large number of specific principles of justice with universal applicability. Reinhold Niebuhr is not a defender of natural law as is generally understood, but neither would he ascribe to a belief that the rights derived from natural law are, to use Bentham's phrase, "nonsense upon stilts."[28] Bentham's view that there are no rights apart from what the positive law gives the citizen certainly runs counter not only to the Stoics and the Judeo-Christian heritage but also to the philosophy of John Locke, which was foundational to the United States.

John Locke writes in his Second Treatise of Government:

> The State of Nature has a Law of Nature to govern it, which obliges every one: And Reason, which is that Law, teaches all Mankind, who will but consult it, that being all equal and independent, no one ought to harm another in his Life, Health, Liberty, or Possessions. For Men being all the Workmanship of one Omnipotent, and infinitely wise Maker; All the Servants of one Sovereign Master, sent into the World by his order and about his business, they are his Property, whose Workmanship they are, made to last during his, not one another's Pleasure.[29]

Thus we see here the theistic strain in the philosophy of a person who made a major impact on the development of American society. (It should be noted that the gist of Locke's position was to grant to people rights from God to illustrate the lack of any special rights from God to the sovereign.) As can be seen, Locke's position is embodied in the familiar words of the Declaration of Independence:

> We hold these truths to be self-evident, that all men are created equal; that they are endowed by their Creator with certain unalienable rights; that among these are life, liberty, and the pursuit of happiness. That, to secure these rights, governments are instituted among men, deriving their just powers from the consent of the governed; . . .

In writing these words Thomas Jefferson not only picked up on the theme of the transcendent source of law and government but also made that source a continuing means for critiquing the society in which one lived.

The idea of consent of the governed as the source of legitimacy of a government was not original with Jefferson. It is found in Locke's idea of tacit consent as well as in Richard Hooker's writing and sermons.[30]

In addition to these philosophical and theological foundations for Americans' understanding of rights, the impact of Protestant churches, although not uniform, is felt in activist movements for the abolition of slavery, civil rights, and antiwar activities. Revulsion over Nazi war crimes provided a stimulus for American Christians, as well as others, to see that human rights were on the agenda at the establishment of the United Nations as well as in various international contexts.[31] Of course it was not until 1948, with the adoption by the United Nations General Assembly of the Universal Declaration of Human Rights, that the scope of international concern for human rights was demonstrated.

A consequence as well as a cause of the struggle for religious liberty (promoted by, among others, certain Protestant groups) was the social space occupied by the church vis-à-vis the government. As the major nongovernmental institution, the church claimed and received a legitimate space within the society. By maintaining a separate space, the church expanded the space for non-religious groups. Max Stackhouse writes:

> The "rights" of these intermediary institutions and nongovernmental organizations are rooted in the fundamental claim that the social space occupied by the church is not to be violated because it is sacred. Individual rights in the American tradition articulated under the impact of these groups, is most profoundly understood to mean the right of the

person to participate in such groups. It is precisely such groups which articulate the source and norm of human dignity, practically empower persons to care for the neighbor, and act to defend the rights of individuals when they are thought to be compromised by governmental or corporate or ethnic discriminations—claiming that they are "members" with equal standing in a more universal community. . . . This . . . is the decisive root of American civil liberties and civil rights. These group rights reflect the basic understanding of what it means to be human, and thus what human rights should be at their deepest.[32]

In both their intellectual and activist manifestations, the Protestant churches have met resistance to their conceptions of human rights, but little effective denial of the churches' right to attempt to influence political policies or the culture generally. In part this may be the result of the dominance of society by a certain segment of the Protestant community. There is some indication that the closeness between the culture and that segment of the Protestant community is dwindling.[33]

In a discussion that seeks to define human rights and delineate their sources one should note the debate surrounding their existence and the concern that they represent either Western imperialism or a fictitious universalism or both. The debate and direction of this student's answer to the charges of Western imperialism and false universalism are pointed to by Sumner Twiss, professor of religious studies at Brown University, and Bruce Grelle, professor of religious studies at California State University, when they write,

Despite the common perception that human rights are simply an outgrowth and entailment of Western assumptions about human nature and moral rationality, it is a fact that the Universal Declaration was reached through a pragmatic process of negotiation between representatives of different nations and cultural traditions. While it may be true that Western representatives had the upper hand in this process, the simple fact remains that pragmatic negotiation between differing views about the subject matter was the process of choice, not theorizing about matters of moral knowledge, political philosophy, or even jurisprudence. Moreover, this pragmatic approach has continued to characterize the drafting and adoption of subsequent human rights covenants, conventions, and treaties. We need to ask, therefore, what this process implies or otherwise suggests about the nature, status, and justification of human rights, and the answer should be somewhat reassuring to those who worry about the hegemony of a particular ideology in human rights.[34]

The adoption of the Universal Declaration of Human Rights met opposition during the United Nations debates along the lines of the imperialism suggested, but even those most vigorously critical, most notably the Soviet Union, did no more than abstain to show its disapproval. The United Nations General Assembly adopted the Universal Declaration December 10, 1948, with a vote of 48 to 0. Poland, Byelorussia, Czechoslovakia, the Ukraine, Yugoslavia, South Africa, Saudi Arabia, and the Soviet Union abstained.[35] Yet even more significant for the question of universalism is the increasing role played by non-Western states in obtaining international recognition of social and economic rights via international agreements. Thus increasingly, "No one cultural tradition is the sole source of human rights concerns."[36] It can be argued that since these rights represent no more than the result of political bargaining they can hardly claim strong moral standing within the community of nations or with the individuals that make up that community. Yet this argument as to the "sacredness" or moral commitment generated by political negotiation may misrepresent or minimize how non-religionists view the evolution of public morality. Instead of representing merely some minimal moral understanding of human rights claims, politically negotiated human rights understandings may represent a revelation of foundational moral claims. It is in this spirit that Imre Szabo, professor at the University of Budapest, has written:

In my opinion, human rights can be "deduced" solely from the social relations from which they have arisen. Putting it bluntly, I personally am hostile to any theory, any explanation, based on so-called natural law. Law founded on reason is pure fiction, as is the assumed existence of a social contract. On the other hand, the economic development, and, correlatively, the political development specific to the 15th and 16th centuries is by no means a fiction since it corresponds to the real development of society. It is this evolution which is at the root of the demand for freedom—above all, economic freedom—in the face of feudal bondage; it was by virtue of this evolution that freedom was postulated and, more particularly, that equality before the law was asserted, in the face of the system of feudal privileges. These needs on the part of society assumed the form of natural law as they were presented as eternal needs. On this account, the relations between natural law and positive law appeared to be the relations between needs and reality, that is to say, positive law as it was subsequently established.[37]

That the author here is writing as one living under the domination of the Soviet Union may or may not be relevant to the main point—that strong moral claims can result from political negotiation deduced from a social situation.

This is to suggest that the question of the universal character of human rights is becoming less of an issue with each new generation of rights agreements. For those of us who look toward our religious heritage for support for human rights, the pragmatic deduction of human rights from a situation may not generate enough of a commitment to human rights. Yet the longings for recognition of human dignity may reveal God's action in history even if the action is not attributed to God.

What we see is a commingling of traditions that have influenced the way people think about human rights. One strand is that of the ancient Greek philosophers, another is pre-Enlightenment and Enlightenment thought, and a third is the Judeo-Christian tradition, both intellectual and activist. From the theory of natural law come concepts of natural rights, which in turn become human rights. The idea of human rights has taken on a certain life of its own, that is, people from non-Western traditions have made strong moral claims, couched as human rights, that have found expression in politically negotiated agreements. At the global level all of these factors need to be taken into account in understanding human rights. From the American perspective, there has been an effective commingling of each of these strands for understanding human rights *except* for the rights promoted by non-Western traditions. In addition to being a current in the stream of American understanding of human rights, the Protestant churches have been a part of the cultural formation of an American creed. It is this creed, with its close relationship to human rights, that connects American understanding of human rights with the Protestant church's ability to present its policy positions in a pluralistic context. It is to the subject of the American creed that we now turn.

Protestant Churches and the American Creed

The purpose of this section is to show that the Protestant churches were influential in establishing a common American creed, which essentially represents Americans' understandings of the basis for human rights. A second purpose of this section is to show that the American creed animates foreign policy and sets the parameters of political discourse in America.

The variety of religious convictions and denominations in America facilitated the establishment of religious liberty in the United States. While the dominant religious emphasis in colonial America was a pervasive Puritanism as modified by Evangelicalism, the impact of rational religion and Enlightenment philosophy on the Declaration of Independence and the preamble to the Constitution is well established. Enlightenment philosophy, liberal religion, and Calvinist religion manifested themselves in the form the new nation took, and they also helped to create a political creed. As Winthrop Hudson, professor of church history at Colgate Rochester Divinity School, points out, the religious pluralism of the United States was a pluralism of religious bodies—denominations—that held a common understanding of Christian faith. In addition there was a "religion of the republic" which was not pluralistic.[38] Hudson further states:

> The religion of the churches and the religion of the republic existed side by side. Since they were regarded as mutually supportive, the distinction between them was often blurred. Still the operating assumption was that the nation had its own independent religious vocation.[39]

(As we will see in the final section of this chapter, there is currently deep concern that the "religion of the republic," to the extent this exists any longer, and traditional religion are not mutually supportive.) This "religion of the republic" may or may not fit the definition of religion, but it seems the sociologist Gunnar Myrdal identifies the same phenomena as the "American Creed." Myrdal writes:

> Still there is evidently a strong unity in this nation and a basic homogeneity and stability in its valuations. Americans of all national origins, classes, regions, creeds, and colors, have something in common: a social *ethos*, a political creed. It is difficult to avoid the judgment that this "American Creed" is the cement in the structure of this great and disparate nation.[40]

According to Myrdal, America has "the *most explicitly expressed* system of general ideals in reference to human interrelations,"[41] when compared to every other country in Western civilization. The main norms of the American creed, belief in equality and in the rights to liberty, have their roots in the Enlightenment and in Christianity, "particularly as it took the form in the colonies of various lower class Protestant sects."[42]

This democratic American creed draws significantly from Protestant Christianity. Myrdal makes this point when he writes:

> The basic teaching of Protestant Christianity is democratic. We are all poor sinners and have the same heavenly father. The concept of natural rights in the philosophy of Enlightenment corresponded rather closely with the ideal of moral law in the Christian faith. . . . Religion is still a potent force in American life. . . . American scientific observers are likely to get their attentions fixed upon the process of progressive secularization to the extent that they do not see this main fact, that America probably is still the most religious country in the Western world. Political leaders are continuously deducing the American Creed out of the Bible.[43]

The fact that political leaders deduce the American creed out of the Bible indicates, to some extent, the usability of religious language. As will be elaborated in the third part of this chapter, religious language, even from the point of view of the public faith, is limited by the concept of separation of church and state.

The nature of the creed has important implications for public policy generally and U.S. human rights foreign policy in particular. Americans, as will be shown, tend to see themselves as the promoters of human rights.

That is, Americans tend to believe that the country's foreign policy should reflect their concern for human rights. Such a foreign policy is a natural reflection of how Americans perceive their country and, at least earlier in its history, what Americans perceived the nation's destiny to be. The norms of the American creed—belief in equality and in the rights to liberty—encourage, at least ideally, equal access to the public square. The most casual observer of American society will note that debate about policy in many instances seems to take for granted equal opportunity for persons to engage in public policy debate. It should not be surprising that Dr. Martin Luther King Jr., in his famous "I Have a Dream" speech, with its religious references, referred to the norms of the American creed to challenge the political establishment to act on behalf of civil rights.

While there was no particular denomination of the American Protestant community that defined the American creed, a general Protestant theology was significant in shaping the creed and the Declaration of Independence. It is interesting to note that three founders who would not be easily identified with any particular religious group, Thomas Jefferson, John Adams and Benjamin Franklin, "were as vigorous as any clergyman in asserting that the United States had come into being as a grand design of Providence" to emancipate mankind from slavery all over the earth.[44] In elaborating on this public faith Hudson notes:

> This faith of the new republic was neither sectarian nor parochial. Its roots were Hebraic. Its explication was cast in Hebraic metaphors—chosen people, covenanted nation, Egyptian bondage, promised land. Its eager millenial expectation was expressed in the vivid imagery of the Hebrew prophets. Its potentially unbridled exuberance was kept in partial check by an Hebraic awareness that divine displeasure could quickly bring divine judgment upon the nation. Nor was the faith of the republic parochial. Members of the Revolutionary and post-Revolutionary generation frequently referred to themselves as "citizens of the world." The blessings they had won were blessings which of right belonged to all men.[45]

Three points should be made here about this characterization of the public faith. First, simply because Protestants were more numerous than other religious groups, especially during the colonial era, the main conduit of the metaphors were the Protestant churches and their Bibles. Second, the "Hebraic awareness that divine displeasure could . . . bring divine judgment upon the nation" is a theme of the political realism of Reinhold Niebuhr. (It should be noted that while this theme is not exclusive to Niebuhrian ethics, because of his emphasis on the persistence and pervasiveness of sin, Niebuhr's realism seems to make this point more powerfully than liberal ethicists usually do. This point will be elaborated in the next chapter.) Third, the emphasis on Providence and the universality of the blessings that Americans enjoyed would have a significant impact on U.S. foreign policy.

The righteousness inherent in the American creed, generated in part by religion, has made an impact on U.S. foreign policy. American foreign policy has alternated between isolationism and messianism, in part because of its religious heritage. As the late Harvard political theorist Louis Hartz has written:

> We have been able to dream of ourselves as emancipators of the world at the very moment that we have withdrawn from it. We have been able to see ourselves as saviors at the very moment that we have been isolationists.[46]

Of course Hartz was making the point that American society, because of its experience, was not a revolutionary society but a liberal one, growing out of a lack of feudal experience. Americans are born free, and the society has little point of identification with other nations of the world who have had to go through a democratic revolution in order to attain the liberal values Americans are born with. This experience of "Americanism" has had a dual life on the world plane, according to Hartz.

> First of all, from the time of Jefferson onward . . . it has been characterized by a strong isolationist impulse: the sense that America's very liberal joy lay in the escape from a decadent Old World that could only infect it with its own diseases. This was the spirit that pervaded most men even during the revolutionary age of American history. And yet, in the twentieth century, "Americanism" has also crusaded abroad in a Wilsonian way, projecting itself headlong over the strange and ancient societies of Europe and Asia. The explanation is actually not hard to find. Embodying an absolute moral ethos, "Americanism," once

it is driven on to the world stage by events, is inspired willy-nilly to reconstruct the very alien things it tries to avoid. Its messianism is the polar counterpart of its isolationism, which is why Harding and Wilson are both "Americanist" thinkers, and why, as Mr. George Kennan has recently noted, Americans seem to oscillate between fleeing from the rest of the world and embracing it with too ardent a passion. An absolute national morality is inspired either to withdraw from "alien" things or to transform them: it cannot live in comfort constantly by their side.[47]

The desire to maintain moral purity manifests itself as either the desire to "evangelize" the rest of the world or to withdraw from it.

The close identification of the churches with the public faith has made it easy to enlist church support. In what Robert Bellah considers one of two moments in U.S. history when churches spoke significantly to U.S. foreign policy, the Protestant churches took on the task of the total evangelization of the world in the early nineteenth century. This American missionary enterprise from the very beginning was concerned to spread not just the gospel itself, but the peculiar blessings of American civil and religious liberty.[48] The extent to which the U.S. government encouraged this effort is open to question, but the effect was still the same, developing support for America's understanding of freedom.

When World War I broke out, the government was concerned to enlist the support of the churches.[49] Religious liberty, as expressed by the phrase "separation of church and state," was certainly an expression of the concern for freedom and equality embodied in the American creed; but most of the Protestant churches could hardly have been more supportive of the U.S. government during World War I than if they had been a state church. The support took a variety of forms. Many churches became recruiting stations, and the clergy often sold Liberty Bonds. The major denominations had independent war work commissions, and the Federal Council of Churches encouraged pastors to organize War Savings Clubs among their Sunday School children and young people.[50]

After World War I, in reaction to their vehement support of the war effort, the churches began passing resolutions renouncing war. In 1924 alone hundreds of these resolutions were passed by denominations large and small. The pacifist movement of the twenties and thirties is credited with modifying the vehemence of church support of World War II (as seen in the more respectful treatment of conscientious objectors by clergy in World War II).[51]

As was seen in the testimony of William Wipfler, more recent church witnessing on foreign policy has challenged, albeit modestly, the American sense of virtue in promoting human rights, and thus challenged a significant feature of our American creed. The letter from Dwain Epps to Rep. Millicent Fenwick did the same thing, in a less detailed way.

Two rather recent documents dealing with the nuclear arms race and nuclear war, the National Conference of Catholic Bishops' *The Challenge of Peace: God's Promise and Our Response* and the United Methodist Council of Bishops' *In Defense of Creation: The Nuclear Crisis and a Just Peace*, contain criticism and express concern over nuclear weapons and war, but no radical critique of the American creed. Perhaps that would have seemed beyond the scope of the documents or perhaps it seemed unnecessary to the issue and unduly provocative given the intent of the essays.

Thus we have an American creed drawn from Enlightenment philosophy and religious, primarily Protestant, roots. The Christian churches, while occasionally calling into question the righteousness Americans attach to themselves in promoting their creed, nevertheless, are predominantly supportive of that creed. As was seen, one element in the public faith is religious liberty, and what that means in how churches raise ethical issues will be seen in the next section of this chapter dealing with Christian realism and religious language in the public square.

Christian Realism, Religious Language, and the Public Square

Will Herberg, in explaining how religious unity operates in the United States, wrote:

> Religion is integral to Americanism as currently understood. "Recognition of the Supreme Being," President Eisenhower declared early in 1955 in his address launching the American Legion's "Back to God" campaign, "is the first, the most basic, expression of Americanism. Without God, there could be no American form of government, nor an American way of life." In uttering these words, Mr.

Eisenhower was speaking for the great mass of American people and affording an important insight into one aspect of contemporary American religiosity. The religious unity of American life implies an institutional and ideological pluralism. The American system is one of stable coexistence of three equi-legitimate religious communities grounded in the common culture-religion of America.[52]

This statement not only ties religion to the American civil society, but also exemplifies a president's use of religious language in public address. The institutional and ideological pluralism implied by the "religious unity of American life" implies itself a public faith and a mode of operation that is consistent with that public faith.

President Eisenhower's use of religious language in the above quotation is but one of numerous examples that could be used to prove the public acceptability of using that language for political purposes in the public square. To say this is not meant to suggest that religion is "used" by politicians, although it may be, but that religious perspectives have a legitimate role to play in informing policy. As Kent Greenawalt, university professor at Columbia University, has written:

Religious convictions of the sort familiar in this (U.S.) society bear pervasively on people's ethical choices, including choices about laws and government policies. This thought is a critical one for most of the rest of this book because, if it is true, a citizen's reliance on religious convictions is inapt only if (1) the religious convictions themselves are wrong, or (2) they merely replicate what is otherwise discoverable by means more consonant with notions of liberal democracy, or (3) they are disqualified by some aspect of liberal democracy or its underlying principles.[53]

The second point made here, by this former professor of jurisprudence, seems to imply that religious convictions are inherently less consonant with notions of liberal democracy. Whether or not this is true, it is important to keep in mind that religious convictions, to the extent liberal democracy is grounded in Christian faith, must not be disqualified by some "aspect of liberal democracy or its underlying principles."

Religious language either in tone or in substance can express convictions that are destructive of liberal democracy. Consequently, not just for practical reasons of effectiveness, churches must understand the implications of their positions for liberal democratic society. The extent to which religion has been instrumental in forming the American creed may reinforce in the churches the tolerance and sensitivity necessary for action in a liberal democracy. It would be ironic, in a study on how churches seek to promote human rights internationally, to find that by their methods or arguments churches denied human rights in the United States.

Probably because Niebuhr's realism grew out of the formerly dominant mainline Protestant culture, Christian realism is more familiar with and comfortable in the public square than conservative religion. The language of Christian realism reflected an early appreciation for the need to speak in publicly accessible reasons and was able to do so precisely because the culture was not hostile to mainline Protestantism, at the time. This is the view implicit in the comment of Richard Neuhaus, director of the Center on Religion and Society, when he writes, "Those who for so long enjoyed a monopoly on the language of Christian social engagement have been forced to distinguish their engagement from that of other Christian forces in the public arena."[54] Neuhaus identifies mainline Protestants with "those who . . . enjoyed a monopoly on the language of Christian social engagement. . . ." Neuhaus implies that the mainline Protestants today must distinguish themselves from the conservative Protestants in order to get the same access to the public square they had during Niebuhr's time.

Robin Lovin identifies the strengths of Christian realist language in public discourse when he writes, responding to Jeffrey Stout's *Ethics after Babel*, that

> This emphasis on diversity and consensus in moral discourse provides, on its own terms, a minimal answer to Stout's question of what theistic references add to discussion in a secular, pluralistic society in which agreements about religion are generally absent. The minimal answer is that a moral and theological realism of the sort that Reinhold Niebuhr elaborates demonstrates that religious thinking need not be dogmatic or divisive, and that when it is not, it can be admitted to the public discussion along with all the other participants. To Stout, the philosopher of religion who asks what theism contributes to the public discussion, we may respond with Stout, the political philosopher, that the point is not contribution, but participation. If the aim of public

discussion is to identify elements of a consensus to which persons will agree for different reasons, rather than to offer reasons for choices one way or another, there is no reason to exclude those whose reasons may be religious, unless these religious persons, by an intolerant demand for consensus on their own terms, exclude themselves.[55]

While this minimal answer may be less than satisfying, it is not insignificant. The danger to democratic society from religious thinking that is dogmatic and divisive is real. Exemplifying this position Niebuhr wrote:

> It is probably true that the health of a democratic society depends more upon the spirit of forbearance with which each side tolerates the irreducible ideological preferences of the other than upon some supposed scientific resolution of them, because the scientific resolution always involves the peril that one side or the other will state its preferences as if they were scientifically validated value judgments.[56]

The fact that Niebuhr elaborates a non-dogmatic and nondivisive religious thinking obviously would make his arguments stronger from the perspective of a public official who would need to build consensus on policy positions. Since public support is needed to sustain policy, as we saw with Kissinger's policy of détente in the first chapter, how we articulate policy may be as important as the policy articulated in some instances.

The ease with which Christian realism engages in public discourse may be seen not only in Reinhold Niebuhr's activities as a consultant to the State Department's Policy Planning Staff and delegate to the United Nations Educational, Scientific, and Cultural Organization but also through his publications addressed to a well-educated (and secular as well as religious) public.[57] Niebuhr was able to write in a way that appealed to (to use Kent Greenawalt's phrase) "shared premises and publicly accessible reasons." Niebuhr explains the reason for Christian realism attempting to do this when he writes:

> While the negative proof of the Christian truth cannot be transmuted into a positive one, which would compel conviction on purely rational grounds, there is nevertheless a positive apologetic task. It consists in

correlating the truth, apprehended by faith and repentance, to truths about life and history, gained generally in experience. Such a correlation validates the truth of faith insofar as it proves it to be a source and center of an interpretation of life, more adequate than alternative interpretations, because it comprehends all of life's antinomies and contradictions into a system of meaning and is conducive to a renewal of life.[58]

While this statement is directed to the person of faith, Niebuhr's appreciation of truths gained generally in experience allowed him to communicate on the basis of shared premises and publicly accessible reasons. The relationship between revealed religion and natural religion is complex. That is, for Niebuhr a part of the truth revealed in Jesus Christ is accessible without faith. Thus Niebuhr writes,

The Christian doctrine of Christ as the "second Adam," as normative man, is thus a doctrine which hovers between natural and revealed religion. It belongs to natural religion in the sense that any rigorous analysis of the moral life of man will, partially disclose the tangents towards the eternal in all morality. It belongs to revealed religion because it is not possible, without faith, to follow these implications through to their final logical conclusion. Without faith the ethical life of man is always haunted by the skeptical reflection that "a living dog is better than a dead lion," which is to say that all moral imperatives are limited by the survival impulse which lies at the foundation of historical existence.[59]

This partial disclosure of "tangents towards the eternal" allows for cooperation in activities for justice with those outside of a shared faith. It is this appreciation for truths gained generally in experience and the need for humility in front of all truth that prevents Christian realist ethics from making intolerant demands for consensus on its own terms.

Because of its ability to articulate an ethics non-dogmatically and non-divisively, Christian realism enhances the prospects that a society will be tolerant of persons making human rights claims. As noted earlier, Niebuhr in writing about "Augustine's Political Realism" defines moral and political realism as "the disposition to take all factors in a social and political situation, which offer resistance to established norms, into account, particularly the factors of self-interest and power."[60] Such a disposition certainly concerns itself with the moral and political arrogance that claims too much for its own understanding of universal human rights. This concern finds expression in how Christian realism presents its ethical positions in the public square.

When we move beyond the minimal position, suggested by Robin Lovin, of mere participation to influence, then concern over shared premises and publicly accessible reasons becomes even more important. While it may be true for some or even all religionists that being faithful is more important than being effective, being influential is still important to the churches, especially those considered in this study.

At one level, suggested by the quotation from President Eisenhower, religious language itself is not a problem in a democratic society (at least in the United States). Participation, in a democratic society, may be enough, especially since influence is so difficult to determine. Yet even participation requires religious organizations to play by the rules. Tolerance in the process of influencing policy seems to be a given. As the pluralism in American society increases, so does the necessity for clearly understanding the boundaries of discourse.

Christian realist thinking has shown remarkable effectiveness in achieving access to policy makers and thus to policy debate. While we might argue that Christian realism had such access because of the dominant position of mainline Protestant churches, it is likely that such access was the result of its theological, as well as its sociological, position in the society. The liberal nature of the mainline Protestant churches, it could be argued, was just as likely, if not more so, to present policy on the basis of a liberal theological outlook of which Christian realism was so critical. The strengths of Christian realism will be explored more fully in the next chapter.

As indicated in chapter two, it is clear that not all churches, including mainline Protestant churches, speak out of a Christian realist perspective. (The strength of Christian realism in communicating in a pluralistic context has been addressed.) Thus the question continues to arise: How do churches, speaking out of their faith, communicate their ethical convictions in American society? In a society that attempts to live by the American creed of equality and liberty, it should be clear that the church can take public positions out of motives that are not accessible to the general public. It may justify those positions in whatever way it deems necessary. There is little speech that is legally limited. This is one of the fundamental rights of American democratic government. At this point you may recall that public officials, such as President Eisenhower, use language in the public square that might be used in religious contexts. Pragmatically, in seeking support for its positions, churches will probably want to justify their public policy positions with publicly accessible reasons. (It should be kept in mind that public policies get adopted via coalition building, and coalitions are often very disparate groups. The entire coalition need not accept the premises of any single member of the coalition in order to work together to get a policy adopted. The "public" is made up of many "publics" and a large number of people consider themselves religious.)   There is a recurrent concern, as expressed above, that in order to maintain a pluralistic, democratic society churches must be able to justify their public policy positions in ways that reinforce liberal, democratic values. A recent popular book, *The Culture of Disbelief: How American Law and Politics Trivialize Religious Devotion*, by Yale law professor Stephen Carter, emphasizes how concern for separating church and state has led to a privatization of religious conviction and marginalization of religious convictions in public policy debate. Carter believes:

> [There is] a burgeoning strand in American political theory holding that whatever grounds might lead citizens to their political views must be justified in secular terms—that is, without regard to religion—when they enter the public square and urge other citizens to act. . . . The philosophical idea is that even though all of us have differing personal backgrounds and biases, we nevertheless share certain moral premises in common. If we then exclude what we do not have in common, what remains can be the basis for a conversation.[61]

Carter's book refutes the notion that religious convictions cannot be given as a motive for supporting a particular public policy. For this writer, Carter's argument is persuasive. While there may be religious convictions and language that clearly run counter to the spirit of liberal democratic government and a pluralistic society, there is nothing inherent in religious convictions that make them antidemocratic. In fact, the analysis of the

American creed and the development of human rights given would suggest that religion is foundational to democracy and respect for rights.

Whether for the practical reason of coalition-building or the need to allay fears that religious groups are attempting to establish a theocracy, it is important that religious groups learn to justify policy in the public square on the basis of reasons accessible to the public. Historically religious groups have done so. Stephen Carter acknowledges that some of the current concern over religiously based policy advocacy comes from people concerned about the "religious right," people who expressed no similar anxiety when Dr. King was marching for civil rights.[62] Evidence suggests that religious representatives in Washington, conservative as well as liberal, have learned the art of articulating positions with publicly accessible reasons.[63] The data surveyed in chapter three, concerning how mainline Protestant churches have communicated their policy preferences, revealed nothing that would be inappropriate to debate in the public square.

Summary

This chapter has focused on three issues. First, it explored the nature and sources of human rights. Second, it raised the issue of how religion has influenced the development of a political creed, the American creed, capable of cementing diverse elements in a pluralistic society. Third, it assessed the problem that religious groups have of advocating public policy in a pluralistic context.

Human rights were seen to be moral-political claims that an individual has a right to make against a government or society simply because that person is a human being. The sources of human rights are varied. Ancient Greek and Roman thought, Christian thought (expressed by theologians as well as the Bible), and Enlightenment philosophy all have contributed to current understandings of what is meant by the term human rights. In addition, human rights have been deduced from social situations through political negotiation. It was argued that the biblical source for understanding human rights is most significant because of the importance of the transcendent authority of God, but that whatever religionists see as the grounding for human rights, in a pluralistic context, effective advocacy of human rights requires justification with publicly accessible reasons. It was argued that non-Western promotion of human rights via international agreements undermines the criticism that human rights are merely a Western concept foisted on the rest of the world.

The Protestant churches in America were influential in helping to establish an "American creed." This creed has as its main norms concern that equality and liberty be respected. Human rights are an expression of these norms, and Americans self-consciously see the country's role as promoting those rights around the world. Historically, the moral purity associated with a belief in human rights has caused American foreign policy to vacillate between isolationism and "evangelical" involvement in the world. The American creed sets the parameters of discourse over foreign policy, at least in theory. Respect for equality and liberty encourages participation in the public square.

People speaking out of their religious convictions are permitted access to the public square. The realism of Reinhold Niebuhr recognized the moral quality of natural religion as well as the experience-based nature of revealed biblical religion. Out of that recognition Christian realism is able to effectively and faithfully engage in public policy debate in a pluralistic society. While there are numerous "publics" that contribute to public policy, some of whom can be appealed to via religious presuppositions and language, a segment of American public opinion is concerned about the use of religious justifications for public policies. (Even many religious people who are not concerned about religious justification for public policies acknowledge the importance of maintaining a separation of church and state.) Religious advocacy groups should be able to justify their public policy positions on publicly accessible grounds for two reasons: (1) to broaden the base of support for its positions and (2) to reinforce values consistent with a pluralistic, liberal, democratic society. Data drawn on in chapter two indicates a sensitivity to the need for reasons that are publicly accessible. In addition, evaluation of religious lobbying activities indicates such sensitivity as well.

As this chapter has indicated, the impact of the Christian church on U.S. society has been so great that even without deliberate involvement in policy formulation Christian ethics has an impact. With these understandings of how religious groups have historically influenced American society the study now turns to the conclusions to be drawn in the juxtaposition of the role of morality and the facts of human rights policy formulation in regard to the CSCE.

Notes

1. Robert Traer, *Faith in Human Rights: Support in Religious Traditions for a Global Struggle* (Washington, D.C.: Georgetown University Press, 1991), 1.

2. Louis Henkin, "Rights: American and Human," *Columbia Law Review* 79 (April 1979): 405. The contribution of the American experience to the definition of human rights via the Virginia Declaration of Rights in 1776 is identified in Nicholas Lossky, Jose Miguez Bonino, John Pobee, Tom Stransky, Geoffrey Wainwright and Pauline Webb, eds. *Dictionary of the Ecumenical Movement* (Grand Rapids, Mich.: William B. Eerdmans Publishing Company, WCC Publications, 1991), s.v. "Human Rights," by Erich Weingartner.

3. J. E. Hare and Carol B. Joynt, *Ethics and International Affairs* (N.Y.: St. Martin's Press, 1982), 13.

4. Maurice Cranston, "What are Human Rights?" in *The Human Rights Reader*, ed. Walter Laqueur and Barry Rubin (N.Y.: New American Library, A Meridan Book, 1977), 22-23.

5. Robin W. Lovin, "Reexamining Human Rights," *The Christian Century*, August 26September 2, 1981, 831.

6. Henkin, "Rights: American and Human," 408.

7. Henkin, "Rights: American and Human," 410.

8. Morton E. Winston, *The Philosophy of Human Rights* (Belmont, Calif.: Wadsworth Publishing Company, 1989), 7.

9. Rex Martin, "Human Rights and Civil Rights," in Winston, *The Philosophy of Human Rights*, 75.

10. Martin, "Human Rights and Civil Rights," 76.

11. Maurice Cranston, *What Are Human Rights?*, with a preface by Reinhold Niebuhr (N.Y.: Basic Books, Inc., 1962), 1.

12. Winston, *The Philosophy of Human Rights*, 3.

13. Aristotle *Politics* 1252a 15.

14. George H. Sabine, *A History of Political Theory*, 3d ed. (N.Y.: Holt, Rinehart and Winston, 1961), 163.

15. Sabine, *Political Theory*, 164.

16. Sabine, *Political Theory*, 164.

17. Max L. Stackhouse, *Creeds, Society, and Human Rights: A Study in Three Cultures* (Grand Rapids, Mich.: William B. Eerdmans Publishing Company, 1984), 31.

18. Stackhouse, *Creeds, Society and Human Rights*, 31.

19. Foster R. McCurley and John H. Reumann, "Human Rights in the Law and Romans (Series A)," in *Human Rights: Rhetoric or Reality*, ed. George W. Forell and William H. Lazareth (Philadelphia: Fortress Press, 1978), 18-22.

20. Stephen Charles Mott, "The Contribution of the Bible to Human Rights," in *Human Rights and the Global Mission of the Church*, by the Boston Theological Institute (Cambridge, Mass.: Boston Theological Institute, 1985), 6.

21. Michael J. Perry, *Love and Power: The Role of Religion and Morality in American Politics* (N.Y.: Oxford University Press, 1991), 39-40. See also Reinhold Niebuhr, *The Nature and Destiny of Man*, vol. II, *Human Destiny* (N. Y.: Charles Scribner's Sons, 1964), 74-76.

22. John T. McNeill, "Natural Law in the Teaching of the Reformers," *The Journal of Religion* 26 (July 1946): 168.

23. Thomas Aquinas, *Treatise on Law (Summa Theologica, Questions 9097)*, with an introduction by Stanley Parry (Washington, D.C.: A Gateway Edition, Regnery Gateway, 1988), 15. This is the second article in answer to question 91 dealing with objection 3.

24. Ernst Troeltsch, *The Social Teaching of the Christian Churches* vol. 1, trans. Olive Wyon, with an introduction by H. Richard Niebuhr (Chicago: University of Chicago Press, 1981), 257.

25. See Perry's *Love and Power*, pages 30-31, for a defense of religious as well as political pluralism.

26. Reinhold Niebuhr, *Faith and History: A Comparison of Christian and Modern Views of History* (N.Y.: Charles Scribner's Sons, Macmillan Publishing Company, 1949), 188-89.

27. Niebuhr, *Faith and History*, 194.

28. *The Works of Jeremy Bentham*, published under the superintendence of his executor John Bowring, vol. 2, "Anarchical Fallacies: Being an Examination of the Declaration of Rights Issued during the French Revolution" (N.Y.: Russell and Russell, Inc., 1962), 501.

29. John Locke, *Two Treatises of Government*, a critical edition with an introduction and apparatus criticus by Peter Laslett (N.Y.: The New American Library, 1965), 311.

30. Richard Hooker, *Of the Laws of Ecclesiastical Polity: Preface, Book I and Book VIII*, ed. Arthur Stephen McGrade (N.Y.: Cambridge University Press, 1994), 90, 143.

31. Henkin, *Rights: American and Human*, 407-8.

32. Stackhouse, *Creeds, Society, and Human Rights*, 52.

33. Stephen L. Carter, *The Culture of Disbelief: How American Law and Politics Trivialize Religious Devotion* (N.Y.: Basic Books, 1993), 57.

34. Sumner B. Twiss and Bruce Grelle, "Human Rights and Comparative Religious Ethics: A New Venue," in *The Annual of the Society of Christian Ethics 1995*, ed. Harlan Beckley (Boston, Mass.: The Society of Christian Ethics, 1995), 31.

35. Peter Meyer, "The International Bill: A Brief History" in *The International Bill of Human Rights*, with a foreword by Jimmy Carter, an afterword by Adolfo Perez Esquivel, and an introduction by Tom J. Farer (Glen Ellen, Calif.: 1981), xxxi.

36. Twiss and Grelle, "Human Rights and Comparative Religious Ethics," 32.

37. Imre Szabo, "Historical Foundations of Human Rights and Subsequent Developments," in *The International Dimensions of Human Rights*, ed. Karel Vasak and Philip Alston (Westport, Conn.: Greenwood Press for Unesco, 1982), 15.

38. Winthrop S. Hudson, *Religion in America: An Historical Account of the Development of American Religious Life*, 2d ed. (N.Y.: Charles Scribner's Sons, 1973), 92, 9495, 110-11.

39. Hudson, *Religion in America*, 110-11.

40. Gunnar Myrdal with the assistance of Richard Sterner and Arnold Rose, *An American Dilemma: The Negro Problem and Modern Democracy*, Twentieth Anniversary Edition (N.Y.: Harper and Row Publishers, 1962), 5.

41. Myrdal, *An American Dilemma*, 5.

42. Myrdal, *An American Dilemma*, 89.

43. Myrdal, *An American Dilemma*, 10-11.

44. Hudson, *Religion in America*, 112.

45. Hudson, *Religion in America*, 112.

46. Louis Hartz, *The Liberal Tradition in America: An Interpretation of American Political Thought since the Revolution*, with an introduction by Tom Wicker (N.Y.: Harcourt Brace Jovanovich Publishers, 1991), 38.

47. Hartz, *The Liberal Tradition*, 285-86.

48. Robert N. Bellah, "Religious Influences on United States Foreign Policy," chap. in *American Character and Foreign Policy*, ed. Michael P. Hamiliton (Grand Rapids, Mich.: William B. Eerdmans Publishing Company, 1986), 53-56.

49. Ray H. Abrams, *Preachers Present Arms: The Role of American Churches and Clergy in World Wars I and II, with Some Observations on the War in Vietnam* (Scottdale, Pa.: Herald Press, 1969), 79.

50. Abrams, *Preachers Present Arms*, 70, 81, 83, 152.

51. Abrams, *Preachers Present Arms*, 234, 269.

52. Will Herberg, *Protestant-Catholic Jew: An Essay in American Religious Sociology* (Garden City, N.Y.: Anchor Books Doubleday and Company, Inc., 1960), 25859. Herberg here quotes Eisenhower from an Associated Press account in the *New York Herald Tribune*, February 22, 1955.

53. Kent Greenawalt, *Religious Convictions and Political Choice* (N.Y.: Oxford University Press, 1988), 30.

54. Richard John Neuhaus, *The Naked Public Square: Religion and Democracy in America*, 2d ed. (Grand Rapids, Mich.: William B. Eerdmans Publishing Company, 1984), 43.

55. Robin W. Lovin, *Reinhold Niebuhr and Christian Realism* (Cambridge, U.K.: Cambridge University Press, 1995), 55.

56. Niebuhr, *Christian Realism and Political Problems*, 90-91.

57. Charles C. Brown, *Niebuhr and His Age: Reinhold Niebuhr's Prophetic Role in the Twentieth Century* (Philadelphia: Trinity Press International, 1992), 148.

58. Niebuhr, *Faith and History,* 165.

59. Reinhold Niebuhr, *The Nature and Destiny of Man,* vol. II, *Human Destiny* (N.Y.: Charles Scribner's Sons, 1964), 75-76.

60. Niebuhr, *Christian Realism and Political Problems*, 119.

61. Carter, *The Culture of Disbelief*, 54-55.

62. Carter, *The Culture of Disbelief*, 64.

63. Allen D. Hertzke, *Representing God in Washington: The Role of Religious Lobbies in the American Polity* (Knoxville: University of Tennessee Press, 1988), 44, 193.

Chapter 5

Conclusions and Summary

The thesis of this work is that there is a role for Christian ethics in the development of foreign policy in general and human rights policy in particular. Concretely, the thesis, as applied to the human rights provisions of the Helsinki Final Act, is that a Christian realist perspective would encourage promotion of human rights without unduly sacrificing other interests and values. It has been argued that this Niebuhrian realism provides a more adequate approach to formulating foreign policy than either an idealistic approach or an approach based on other forms of realism. In light of the thesis the purpose of this chapter is not merely to summarize the data presented in the previous chapters but also to integrate the theoretical discussion of ethics with the historical discussion of CSCE. The conclusions of such integration will address the following interrelated questions: What, if any, is the "abiding truth" in the unique experience of CSCE that can be gleaned about the role of Christian ethics in the development of U.S. foreign policy? To what extent were the factors that led to the human rights understanding in CSCE from 1973 to 1980 unique? And, does the dialectic inherent in the Christian realist ethical perspective provide an adequate framework for analyzing all U.S. foreign policy dealing with human rights?

In addressing the last question the study will analyze the strengths and weaknesses of Christian realism in promoting human rights. This analysis will be based on a critique of David Little's discussion of Niebuhr in "The Recovery of Liberalism: *Moral Man and Immoral Society* Sixty Years Later."[1] Little's critique is more detailed and more explicitly aimed at Niebuhr's writings than other criticisms already examined and as such provides more insight into Niebuhr.

In answering the above questions about U.S. policy it should be kept in mind that a democratic society has been presupposed. That is, since the book has dealt with foreign policy formation in the United States, it has assumed not only a right of citizen participation but also a likelihood of citizen involvement. Such involvement, and therefore such conclusions as are drawn from this study, might also apply in other democracies. To the extent that democracy sets the norm for this student the conclusions are normative.

CSCE, Human Rights, and Christian Realism

From what has been said in the first chapter, it is clear that the impetus for holding the Conference on Security and Cooperation in Europe came from the Soviet Union. Initially, in developing the Final Act, it was the West Europeans, in particular the British, who pushed hardest for the human rights provisions. The United States during the Nixon administration was concerned chiefly with bilateral relations with the Soviet Union and thus attempted to play down human rights, fearing too much emphasis in that area would undermine détente. From the point of view of the Nixon administration the establishment of the CSCE was a concession to Brezhnev. The United States acquiesced to the West European leadership on human rights. After Nixon's fall and America's growing domestic dissatisfaction with détente, Kissinger at key points pressed the Soviets on human rights in the CSCE. The Final Act embodied the compromises that are inevitable in a negotiation that includes sovereign nations. The Final Act represents an enormous achievement of diplomacy in that thirty-five nations developed and signed it. Yet the Final Act was in one sense only the beginning of the CSCE. The importance of the CSCE as a process whereby nations would hold each other accountable on human rights was really only hinted at in the Accord itself.

With the advent of the Carter administration one finds the difficulty with making or attempting to make human rights the central thrust of a nation's foreign policy. While Soviet human rights activists applauded President Carter's support for human rights, President Carter and Secretary of State Vance soon discovered the Soviets would link human rights rhetoric and efforts with progress on nuclear arms reduction. To put it another way, if the United States insisted on promoting human rights, the Soviets would refuse to come to agreement on reducing nuclear arms. When the Carter administration realized this, it realistically modified its position. Nevertheless, U.S.-Soviet relations continued to deteriorate throughout President Carter's term in office.

The Final Act and the CSCE process itself owe their existence to the fact that the Soviet Union wanted its domination of Eastern Europe legitimated in an international agreement that would approximate the stature of a peace treaty ending World War II. In order to come to an agreement on the Final Act, the two Germanies had to be assured that the Final Act would allow for peaceful adjustment of international boundaries.

Because the Basket III provisions were more specific than, say, the Universal Declaration of Human Rights, they provided an effective instrument for measuring compliance with the Accord and, thereby, encouraged activities in the Soviet Union and East Europe for democratization. Even so the more general human rights provisions of the Final Act, found in the "Declaration of Principles," also helped the process.

From the perspective of foreign policy development the access of the public to the CSCE process via the Commission on the CSCE proved valuable. The joint U.S. Senate and House of Representatives Commission might have proved cumbersome to the executive branch of government, but it provided a forum for those East European dissidents needing to give evidence of noncompliance. When the U.S. administration failed to give leadership on human rights, the Commission heightened the importance of human rights.

Although American public opinion tended not to view the Final Act or the CSCE favorably, neither did it like the realpolitik of Henry Kissinger.

The criticism of Kissinger's foreign policy came from both the left and the right. Carter, with his emphasis on human rights in foreign policy, was able to capitalize on the disenchantment in his bid for the presidency. In the immediate post-Watergate, post-Vietnam era the American people looked with a sense of urgency for moral direction from their president. This sense of urgency grew out of a distrust of government that pervaded American society. The Carter human rights policy arguably helped restore in the American people their faith in their own, as well as the American government's, virtue.

In this context the Protestant churches sought to witness to their faith. It should not be surprising that the churches would be cautious about supporting policies that the government adopted. From a theological perspective, including but not limited to Christian realism, prophetic religion must always be critical of the power and policies of government, no matter which government. In addition, promoting international human rights during the Cold War between the United States and the Soviet Union had been seen as a weapon in that war. Quite naturally the Protestant churches did not want to aid the U.S. position on human rights if in doing so the Cold War would be transformed into a hot war. Another reason suggested as to why mainline Protestant churches might be reluctant to press human rights issues is their reluctance to jeopardize ties with churches in the Soviet Union.

This is not to suggest that mainline Protestant churches had nothing to say on human rights. In fact the research presented indicates that the churches had a great deal of support for human rights policy, but in venues other than U.S.-Soviet relations. With regard to the CSCE both the World Council of Churches and the National Council of Churches supported human rights. In particular the concern of the WCC was religious freedom, but the focus tended to be on their churches rather than on a nation's foreign policy. That is, mainline Protestant bodies tended to look at what churches taught about human rights to their church members rather than taking a position in the political arena.

Did the churches adopt a Niebuhrian approach to human rights foreign policy? The answer seems to be no and yes. The answer is no in that the data present no clear statement of debt to Reinhold Niebuhr or Christian realism. (It would have been somewhat surprising to have found explicit attribution to any one thinker or school of thought in public testimony.) There is no conscious appropriation explicit in the testimony of church officials to policymakers. This may not be surprising, since Niebuhr was widely known as a major proponent of the values that led to the Cold War. He was too identified with hostility toward the Soviet Union. The mainline churches sought to encourage détente and human rights.

On the other hand, if one looks at the categories and concerns of the churches, yes, the mainline churches did reflect the issues and opinions found in Niebuhrian realism. The emphasis on humility in promoting human rights is, as has been shown, consistent with Christian realism. The question is raised as to what extent the U.S. abides by the terms of the Accord. The concern that Niebuhr expressed, that a nation should operate in the national interest but define that interest in a way that is sensitive to the interests of other nations, is found in testimony representative of the mainline Protestant churches.

The process of détente, if not the word and policy identified with Kissinger and Nixon, was a priority for the churches and for Niebuhr. Détente did not necessarily mean that the values of Western democracies changed, only that the mode of operating with the Soviet Union allowed for more cooperation and encouraged less confrontation. As thought of by Kissinger, if not by all the supporters of détente, détente was a means to carry out containment of communism at a lowered risk of nuclear confrontation. (After the Kissinger-Nixon era, mainline Protestant churches would probably not have called what they sought détente, since it was both more and less than they wanted. It was more than the churches wanted in that it was a means to containment. As a policy, it was less than they wanted because it still allowed a level of military spending and confrontation that was less than ideal.) The credit, to the extent there is "credit" for the churches reflecting a Christian realist approach, stems less from any conscious adoption of Niebuhr's approach than from the insight which that method of analysis brought to the issues. The method of analysis held together the twin values of freedom and peace.

Two caveats should be noted. First, to speak of the beliefs or positions of mainline Protestant churches can be misleading. There is great diversity among the churches of any single denomination or communion as well as among the denominations. Some people would be more likely to acknowledge their dependence upon and acceptance of

Niebuhrian realism than others. Second, it is difficult to maintain the tension between promoting freedom (human rights) and peace (détente), as Niebuhr does in his writings, in a church organization. That is, programmatically an institution might emphasize human rights, on the one hand, or peace, on the other, so that it might not seem to be maintaining both emphases, when in fact it was.

While this book has explored the nature of the CSCE as well as morality and international relations, it would be well to examine more closely the specific role of human rights in foreign policy according to Christian realism. Reinhold Niebuhr did not write extensively on human rights as such but did deal with the concept in other terms. Niebuhr's concern with justice, his attack on communism, and his defense of democracy all make reference to his understanding of human nature and how that nature is related to God. In a 1957 essay entitled "Theology and Political Thought in the Western World" he writes,

> If we fully analyze the complex relation which exists between religious and rational factors in the establishment of justice, we must come to the conclusion that two elements are equally necessary for the solution of the problems of human community. One is a proper reverence for factors and forces which are truly absolute; and the other is a discriminate attitude toward relative and ambiguous factors and forces. As Christians we insist that there be a proper reverence for the absolute factors, which might be enumerated as: (1) The authority of God beyond all human and historic authorities, enabling us to defy those authorities on occasion with a resolute "We must obey God rather than men." (2) The authority of the moral law embodied in the revelation in Christ, which is to be distinguished from any particular version of that law which may have evolved historically, including the different versions of "natural law." (3) The insistence upon the "dignity" of the person which makes it illegitimate for any community to debase the individual into a mere instrument of social process and power and try to obscure the fact of his ultimate destiny, which transcends all historic realities. This acknowledgment of the "dignity" of man must be accompanied in Christian thought by a recognition that this precious individual is also a sinner, that his lusts and ambitions are a danger to the community; and that his rational processes are tainted by the taint of his own interests. (4) Reverence for the "orders" of authority and

social harmony which have actually been established among us, beyond the wisdom of man and frequently by providential workings in which "God hath made the wrath of man to praise him."[2]

As this passage indicates, Niebuhr was concerned not only to show human sinfulness but also human sacredness. There is a standard standing in judgment of human institutions and history. There is a dignity that deserves respect. Though he warns about the corruption of these "absolutes," he lifts them up nevertheless. Even here Niebuhr is aware of the difference between the particular and the universal. That is, he shows himself to be a respecter of the differences between societies, an important point when promoting human rights. As noted, this particular article is dated 1957. Niebuhr's emphasis had shifted over the years in response to fascism and, later, communism. Since at least 1946 Niebuhr saw religion as providing the resources for a long, frustrating struggle against Soviet communism.[3]

Henry Kissinger, a different kind of realist, in a recent article, "Reflections on Containment," described how he saw the American radicals and their challenge to containment, when he wrote that the radicals believed: "Since prejudice, hatred and fear were the root causes of international conflict, the United States had no moral right to intervene abroad until it had banished these scourges from its own society."[4] Niebuhr, like Kissinger, of course, would reject such reasoning because he recognized that all people are sinful and there are no completely moral policies. As Christians we are compelled to act in an ambiguous world. Kissinger continues, "Postulating the moral equivalence of American and Soviet actions became a characteristic of the radical critique throughout the Cold War."[5] Niebuhr, knowing the attractiveness of communism and the power of religion, articulated a critique of authoritarianism of both the left and the right that supports human rights. Niebuhr argued that while the United States is not free from immorality in its policies and actions it nevertheless is morally preferable to the Soviet Union. For Niebuhr, the problem with Soviet communism was not its atheism but its idolatrous nature.

Even before Niebuhr articulated his objections to the Soviet Union and its foreign policies, he recognized the danger inherent in Marxism. In 1944 Niebuhr wrote, "The social harmony of which Marxism dreams would eliminate the destructive power of human freedom; but it would also destroy the creative possibilities of human life."[6] The importance of freedom as expressed here is not simply spiritualized, as for Martin Luther, but is concretized to be applied in a social context. Niebuhr wrote,

> A free society is justified by the fact that the indeterminate possibilities of human vitality may be creative. Every definition of the restraints which must be placed upon these vitalities must be tentative; because all such definitions, which are themselves the products of specific historical insights, may prematurely arrest or suppress a legitimate vitality, if they are made absolute and fixed. The community must constantly reexamine the presuppositions upon which it orders its life, because no age can fully anticipate or predict the legitimate and creative vitalities which may arise in subsequent ages.[7]

Note that the free society is justified by human vitality, a characteristic not of one group of people but of humanity. This certainly is a claim against society that seems both universal and ongoing. It is rooted in one's humanity. Thus it can be said that Niebuhr is here writing about what is identified as human rights. The claim is for the widest freedom of human development consistent with the justifiable limits on that freedom a society can make. Thus it seems that the argument is for human rights even though those rights are not, in the context of this discussion, clearly elaborated. (It may be objected here that, from a positivist perspective, such an abstract claim to freedom may represent no claim at all to any specific understanding of human rights. It should be recalled that before human rights are actually political and legal claims they are moral claims.) It can be argued that Niebuhr makes the case for a right to freedom of expression when he writes, "Sometimes new truth rides into history upon the back of an error. An authoritarian society would have prevented the new truth with the error."[8] In this same discussion he even more clearly expresses the universal nature of the morality that underlies freedom and justice when he writes,

> Furthermore the final resource against idolatrous national communities, who refuse to acknowledge any law beyond their power, must be found in the recognition of universal law by individuals, who have a source of moral insight beyond the partial and particular national communities,

which are always inclined to set a premature limit upon man's sense of moral obligation. No world community can ever be created if the full religious height of the individual's freedom over the community is not explored and defended.[9]

At this point a word of caution should be added on two points. First, Niebuhr's defense of democracy outlined above is not a prescription for foreign policy. As much as free societies are to be desired, that does not mean a particular nation's foreign policy can or should be built around promoting democratic countries and human rights to the exclusion of other interests. *The Children of Light and the Children of Darkness* may have bolstered American spirits in the struggle against Germany and Japan in World War II, but it did not define how postwar America should conduct its foreign policy. Second, the universalism expressed above does not necessarily mean that positive law can reflect the moral law in the same way at all places. Differences in the historical and cultural experiences of societies will cause variations in how different countries go about putting what might be called "natural law" concepts into positive law.

In the context of concrete U.S.-Soviet relations, Niebuhr was not always the critic of the Soviet Union one sees in the late 1940s and early 1950s. Prior to 1946 he emphasized in an approving way the Soviet Union's attempt to operationalize equality. He recognized the need to draw upon the moral strengths of democracy in order to wait out the dissipation of Communist fanaticism. His analysis of Soviet communism as a religion is echoed in an article he wrote in 1955,

We must expect the Communist dogma to be preserved, perhaps for ages to come, and the Communist oligarchs to pay lip service to it for many decades. Whether they are true believers or whether skepticism has corroded their souls may be politically irrelevant so long as they recognize that they cannot challenge the dogma upon which their political power rests. But it is not politically irrelevant in the long run, for the corrosion of skepticism among both leaders and followers may prevent proclamation of the "holy war" which we have dreaded so much. In that sense, the "big thaw" may be one of the most important events in contemporary history.[10]

Niebuhr was hostile toward Soviet Communist expansion because of communism's ideological pretensions and its willingness to sacrifice freedom to equality as a principle of justice. In fact, as in so many other contexts, he tried to maintain the principle of equality without turning it into an ideology. Note the following:

> Equality is a transcendent principle of justice and is therefore rightly regarded as one of the principles of natural law. But if a natural law theory insists that absolute equality is a possibility of society, it becomes an ideology of some rebellious group which does not recognize that functional inequalities are necessary in all societies, however excessive they may be in the society which is under attack. If on the other hand functional inequalities are exactly defined the definitions are bound to contain dubious justifications of some functional privileges, possessed by the dominant classes of the culture which hazards the definition.[11]

The concern here is not to let the attempt to establish equality obscure the real and necessary inequalities that exist. The corrective concern is not to acquiesce in unjust inequalities. Thus justice requires that freedom and equality be maintained together. Niebuhrian realism was practical enough to recognize that how a society realizes freedom and equality is a matter of empirical observation.

Mere pronouncements of abstract goals were not enough to indicate the seriousness of a political order in pursuing freedom and equality. Ideologically Niebuhr hoped that the competition between the United States and the Soviet Union would promote justice. The lack of freedom and equality worldwide made human rights for Niebuhr more of a moral ideal than a political reality.[12]

Thus one finds in Niebuhr a concern for human rights grounded in freedom. Human rights might be enhanced by the struggle between the United States and the Soviet Union, if the superpowers could avoid nuclear war. (It should be noted that the Final Act's Basket III provisions did not include the economic rights for which the Soviet Union in most human rights discussions generally argued.) In spite of its theoretical support for social equality, Niebuhr's assessment of Soviet communism's hostility toward freedom led him to be highly critical of the Soviet Union.

David Little argues that while Reinhold Niebuhr assisted in the recovery of liberalism, and thus human rights, he did not go far enough. Dr. Little writes that Niebuhr "drastically misrepresented one important part of liberal theory. Ironically, it is the very part that has, since World War II, been recovered and put to use by the world community in the campaign for universal human rights."[13] Dr. Little's criticism of Niebuhr is, on one level, a criticism of his radical separation between individual and collective morality as expressed in *Moral Man and Immoral Society* and, on another level, a criticism of Niebuhr's understanding of liberalism, in particular the liberalism of John Locke.

On the first level, criticism of Niebuhr's radical separation between individual and collective morality, it should be noted that in later years Niebuhr qualified his position on the separation of the two moralities. Yet even before such qualification of his earlier position Niebuhr had written on the relationship between love and justice, and it was clear that the love we experience on the personal level in the death of Jesus judged (and judges) the justice expressed on the corporate level.[14] Niebuhrian realism, as has been shown, is concerned with morality even in collective situations, such as setting foreign policy.

Little's second level of criticism is more substantial and more difficult to refute. He writes,

> Liberalism is not all of a piece, and it cannot properly be summarized, as Niebuhr repeatedly summarized it, as committed to moral and rational optimism, to the artificiality of community, and to *laissez faire*, the natural identity of interests, and utilitarianism.[15]

John Locke, a liberal, did not believe the things Niebuhr accuses him of, at least not without serious qualification.[16] Niebuhr's lack of appreciation for Locke is less important for the development of human rights than Niebuhr's correct appreciation for the degree to which human rights are the positive expression of what the political context will bear. This is not to suggest that human rights for Niebuhr are not moral claims, but Niebuhr understood that substantive enactment of human rights depends on the political context and that not all governments or societies were based on, or were likely to be based on, a Lockean understanding of the social contract. (This is to suggest that Niebuhr, like Henkin, was aware of the difference between human rights as understood in an American context and human rights seen as an expression of international law.)

At this point should be noted the disagreement between David Little and Louis Henkin. Henkin, in making the distinction between American rights and human rights as currently adopted in the international community, persuasively argues that when Americans support human rights, they do so without always acknowledging that our understanding is within the context of a system of government that owes much to Locke, while human rights internationally are not set in that philosophical context. The result, according to Henkin, is that international human rights documents have a more positive, as opposed to natural, character and therefore are likely to have less standing in any given country than we are used to in the United States.[17] This is a disagreement between Louis Henkin and David Little to the extent that the former sees the promotion of human rights as merely expressions of political agreement unaided by liberal thought and the latter sees liberal theory as "put to use by the world community in the campaign for universal human rights." The distinction between the two is the extent to which the positivist approach predominates over (according to Dr. Henkin) the natural approach (for Dr. Little apparently a much greater factor in the international arena).

No matter how much one might wish human rights might be grounded in a liberal democratic tradition, pressure for human rights in any given state may have to precede development of liberal democratic societies given the small likelihood that societies will become democratic before being forced to recognize human rights. This, of course, suggests just how tenuous is the realization of rights in much of the world. In fact, from the East European experience, or more precisely the Soviet experience, recognition of human rights in a positive legal sense might precede a full appreciation for a liberal democratic government, limited and constitutionally grounded. As Louis Henkin suggests, from the perspective of American experience the separation of human rights from the liberal theory of government seems alien. Clearly, a *de jure* recognition of rights, especially in international law, is no substitute for a *de facto* realization of rights.

Part of what Niebuhr was doing in his writings, though not specifically with regard to Locke, was criticizing a cultural liberalism that manifested the qualities that threatened peace and justice in both the domestic and international realms. A moral and rational optimism would not effectively see and deal with the evil presented by Nazi Germany. A faith in the covenantally created community (manifested in U.S. experience as the Constitution) expressed in the League of Nations Covenant would lead to cynicism as the League was unable to deal with major political crises prior to World War II. And a faith in the natural identity of interests would prevent the United States from addressing adequately the challenge of Soviet communism.

Thus for two reasons Dr. Little's second criticism misses the larger point. Namely, the promotion of human rights is only in part a reflection of Locke's thought. And, the concerns which preoccupied Reinhold Niebuhr are not concerns that are disembodied from either his own or our history.

With this summary of the CSCE experience and human rights from a Christian realist perspective, let us examine the unique features of the CSCE. In analyzing the unique characteristics of the CSCE (and the Final Act) it is hoped that one will discover meaningful constants in the process that will enhance the promotion of human rights.

Uniqueness of the CSCE

As noted in the introduction, the CSCE has been credited with empowering the pro-democracy movements in East Europe, primarily through the human rights provisions of the Final Act. Given the importance attached to the document and process, it is important to learn from the experience what might be imitated or duplicated so as to enhance human rights in other contexts.

To say that the international situation surrounding the development of the Final Act and the negotiations within the CSCE was unique is to state the obvious. "The Helsinki Summit was the high-water mark of the détente era of the 1970s; it was the very symbol of détente, and its most ambitious manifestation."[18] Détente between the United States and the Soviet Union was not a natural state of affairs between the end of World War II and the demise of the Soviet Union. As William Korey noted, "Not since the Congress of Vienna in 1815 had so many foreign ministers gathered under one roof to discuss European issues."[19] The prestige and interest shown by the investment of such high-level delegations indicates the importance the Final Act had for the nations involved. The elaborate and painstaking process of constructing the document signed in 1975 was unusual because of the number of nations as well as the wide scope of subject matter involved. The status of the document in the eyes of many of the nations, not least of which being the USSR, was very high. Given the importance of the Final Act, from the European perspective, the process of the CSCE developed great significance.

The legitimization of boundaries, and the sphere of influence of the Soviet Union, made the document significant for the USSR, and in so doing increased the leverage of the nations pushing the human rights provisions. Whether or not the Soviet Union intended to abide by the human rights provisions of the Final Act, it was compelled to accept them. In the process of the follow-up meetings in Belgrade and Madrid, as well as subsequent meetings in Vienna and Paris, the human rights agenda loomed larger than the Soviet Union anticipated.

From the point of view of setting U.S. foreign policy, the ultimate public involvement via the Commission on Security and Cooperation in Europe was unique. Political realists, such as Hans Morgenthau, may lament the passing of the age of aristocratic diplomacy, but an excellent case can be made that in this particular instance the Commission acted as a positive public catalyst promoting human rights. And in attempting to promote human rights the Commission may have helped in breaking up a totalitarian society threatening to U.S. interests and international peace.

With so much that is contextual in the whole CSCE experience, it may seem difficult to generalize about how to promote human rights in international relations. The liberal internationalist might draw from this experience the conclusion that all that needs to be done to promote human rights is to articulate those rights in such a way as to animate the appropriate public opinion. The realist, on the other hand, might conclude that, as the nations pursued their national interests, they ultimately undermined the Soviet Communist system. Thus for the realist CSCE may reinforce the importance of pursuing the national interest. For the realist the containment of communism was in some sense a means of practicing a new balance of power system. The Christian realist might conclude that some combination of articulation of human rights, review of compliance with those rights, and containment of Soviet expansion at the lowest possible risk of war (détente) brought about the desired outcome. Thus the

Christian realist sees the need to articulate a vision of human freedom while at the same time protecting members of the international system from the hegemonic designs inherent in the pursuit of inordinate national self-interest.

The focus on promoting human rights, as the realists will note, may not in the long run be in keeping with the concept of national interest. Within the context of the CSCE and the Final Act, promoting human rights essentially kept the Soviet Union on the defensive. While the democratic nations overtly encouraged the peoples of Eastern Europe to reveal instances of noncompliance with the human rights provisions of the Final Act, these same democratic nations unconsciously encouraged the erosion of national sovereignty. This internationalization of human rights may come back to haunt these nations if, for example, economic rights ever gain the same status in international law as the political rights articulated in the Final Act. This unintended consequence may be less likely to occur, given the fact that there is no real champion of social justice in the system of states. The liberal democratic worldview is now at least not challenged by any alternative view likely to gain a significant platform in the near term.

Apart from the successful challenge waged by democratic nations against Soviet communism on behalf of human rights, the concept itself, apart from more recent concerns about group rights as human rights, challenges state authority. The national interest may not be the same as it clashes with more individual interests. There may be an increasingly ambiguous concept of national interest as the realm of exclusive "domestic jurisdiction" dwindles. This is not to suggest the imminent demise of the state. It is merely a suggestion that forces may have been encouraged in the CSCE as well as other fora that make it more difficult to define the national interest.

The emphasis here on national interest suggests a realist's bent and calls to mind Lord Palmerston's words that in international relations "there are no permanent friends or permanent enemies; there are only permanent interests."[20] The permanent interests expressed in the Final Act and the CSCE suggest that the Western nations thought a more open Soviet society would be in their interest. Presumably such a Soviet Union would be more peaceful. A decreased threat of war would seem to be in each nation's interest unless a nation sought to change the existing power balance. It might be argued that the promotion of human rights in the CSCE was a means to carry on war via diplomatic means. Yet, as has been pointed out in earlier chapters, foreign policy in the United States certainly, and in other democratic states probably, needs widespread public acceptance of their foreign policies; and one of the most effective ways of obtaining that support is to promote, rhetorically at least, human rights. Thus promotion of human rights is a permanent interest of the United States.

In retrospect it seems the cost for promoting human rights in the CSCE was not too great. Promoting human rights may not always be so inexpensive. For example, the cost for not giving China most favored nation trading status because of human rights violations might have been quite so high had the MFN status not been granted. But going into CSCE the United States did not know what price would be paid. (It might be added that during the course of the next several years relations were strained between the two countries, and fear of nuclear war grew.)

The interest of maintaining peace and promoting freedom may be permanent, but contextual factors may determine the exact nature of the policy. One of the features of the Final Act negotiations that will be characteristic of future negotiations is the ability of a nation not to be seen to want the negotiation too much. The ability of a country to walk away from the negotiation, to end the discussion, gives that state maneuverability it might not otherwise seem to have. If a nation seems to want an agreement too badly, it loses some bargaining power. This lesson may have been learned from observation of the CSCE negotiations, but it could be learned in most any diplomatic setting.

The experience of negotiating the Final Act and the CSCE process were, in terms of this study, complementary but discrete events. Success in writing and getting ratified the Final Act in no way assured the success of the CSCE review process. The Final Act was effective because signatory nations were held accountable to each other. The development of Helsinki Watch groups helped give substance to the CSCE review process. The aspirations represented by the process will no doubt continue to pervade foreign policy and international relations. The methods of diplomacy will continue to reflect the relative power positions of the negotiating nations. But awareness of the uniqueness of the CSCE should fill anyone wishing to duplicate the outcome and determine history's course with great humility.

At this point let us turn to a summary of the role of morality in relation to the CSCE.

The Role of Morality in CSCE

Human rights, as Niebuhr pointed out, are grounded in freedom. That freedom allows the widest possible leeway for each individual human being to develop. In the process of elaborating and executing the Final Act, the universal character of human rights found expression. The moral law, expressed in the language of human rights in the Final Act, animated activists and politicians. The actual language of the document reflected the political realities then existing, and the effectiveness of the process was determined by the evolving political climate. To put this in the pattern of Christian realism, it would be a mistake to make either too much or too little of the power of moral ideals in the setting of the foreign policies and effectiveness of the CSCE.

In relation to foreign policy the role of morality is to avoid moralism. This was a concern of Kissinger and Nixon during the early negotiations on the Final Act. But, as the Christian realist would point out, morality is not merely a cloak for power politics but also a source of power and insight into what is truly in the national interest. Morality's task is to translate the public passion and purpose in a way that avoids confrontation whenever possible. That is, the quality of morality lifted up is prudence. Prudence is not, however, the only characteristic of morality needed in foreign policy.

In regard to the international arena, morality serves to acknowledge the plurality found therein and to encourage the diversity to the greatest extent possible. This is akin to the freedom Niebuhr writes of in relation to the indeterminate human potential. Part of the wisdom of Christian realism is acknowledgement of the anarchic nature of the international arena without exaggerating the anarchy. Within the multicultural setting of international relations morality may help broaden the definition of national interest so as to find common ground on which community may be built. With greater community there will be less resort to violence. An overarching moral sense may animate the building of community while recognizing that the specific content of justice among peoples necessitates dialogue among a multiplicity of moral perspectives. This agenda for morality in international relations may seem broad, but it seems that, deliberately or not, elements of the CSCE process promoted that agenda.

Summary

The thesis of this study is that Christian realism would provide a more effective and appropriate approach to U.S. human rights foreign policy at the CSCE than either liberal idealism or realism as realpolitik. In order to see if mainline Protestant churches might have offered such a Christian realist perspective to policymakers, this book has explored to what extent and how mainline churches attempted to influence U.S. policy.

The first chapter outlined in some detail the various contexts in which the policy was made. The reason for such historic detail was to explore the possible consequences of policy. This is because the strength of Christian realism lies, among other places, in its concern for consequences. This is not meant to suggest that liberal idealism is unconcerned about consequences, but rather if the moral norms promoted by liberal idealism, such as a prohibition on the use of violence, are to be countered it must be demonstrated that the norms themselves may be counterproductive. That is, for example, a policy of consistent pacifism may encourage war, the very thing it seeks to discourage. In the context of CSCE the Niebuhrian realist position would promote a prudent foreign policy since it would maintain consistent concern for détente on the one hand and promotion of human rights on the other. In addition, although it is impossible to conclude with certainty, the awareness of national interest and the power relationship among the nations inherent in realist theory may have made the United States more aware of its human rights leverage vis-à-vis Soviet desire for an agreement. There is no evidence to conclude that insight from Niebuhrian realism would have provided any greater predictability that the Soviet Union would collapse.

The second chapter defined Christian realism and explained the strengths of Christian realism in relation to both liberal idealism and realism in other forms. It was argued that Niebuhrian realism could maintain, via its anthropology, a middle way between an inevitably disappointing utopianism in idealism and a cynicism generated by a realism that would miss opportunities for genuine breakthroughs in international relations.

The third chapter, dealing with mainline Protestant attempts to influence U.S. foreign policymaking, revealed no consistent theological perspective. While there are elements within the testimony of the churches that are consistent with Christian realism, there seems to be as much liberalism as realism. Given the diversity within the churches, if not necessarily among the hierarchies of various denominations, it may not be surprising to find no consistent ethical perspective.

Chapter four sought to illustrate the strengths of Niebuhrian realism in the public square. As Kent Greenawalt pointed out, for religious expression to be apt in the American public square, the religious convictions must not be invalidated by more authentic or true religious convictions, the insights expressed religiously must be able to be expressed in terms of publicly accessible reasons, and the religious expression must not contradict basic democratic principles. By these criteria Niebuhrian realism seems to be apt, although there are those who would question it on theological grounds.

Finally, the last chapter sought to make clear that Niebuhrian realism approached human rights in a way that avoids moralism and the dangers attending that moralism for foreign policy. Nevertheless, this Christian realism posits that justice is informed by love. Christian realism, though sensitive to the diverse historical and political situations of states, suggests the moral law reflected in human rights may result in a greater realization of those rights even though they may not accompany liberal democratic government, as understood in America.

In practice, setting U.S. human rights policy in the CSCE reflected the twin concerns for both the policy of Kissinger and that of President Carter. That is, Kissinger, who was preoccupied with détente, at a later stage in the process became an advocate for human rights and President Carter, initially making human rights the centerpiece of his foreign policy, modified his stance in order to have better relations with the Soviets. Thus, both policies in actuality expressed the tension in practice that Christian realism acknowledged in theory. A virtue of Christian realism is that it displays the theoretical resources to prevent sacrificing either element. The idealism inherent in either seeking to make the world over in our image (i.e., have all other nations adopt human rights as we, in the

United States, understand them) or in seeking to abolish the use of force in international relations (i.e., to the extent détente represented that for Americans) might be modified, though not obliterated, by Christian realism. Mainline Protestant churches manifested a desire for both human rights and détente but revealed no consistently Christian realist stance in their efforts to influence U.S. policy.

A difficulty with arguing for a policy from a Christian realist position is that, because it maintains a polarity that encourages prudence, the policy may seem wedded to the status quo. Another difficulty is that in arguing against moralism and moralistic rhetoric in foreign policy Christian realism may not provide a clear picture of what policy should be adopted in any given context. A policy based on Christian realism may not provide the hope necessary to energize political support within a nation, even though in theory it realizes the importance of such support. Yet, with these concerns in mind, a consistent Christian realist approach seems to offer a framework of analysis which could benefit policymakers concerned with setting U.S. human rights foreign policy.

Notes

1. David Little, formerly a professor of religion at the University of Virginia and currently a research associate at the United States Institute of Peace, delivered this paper at a conference on "Self-Interests and the Common Good: The Problem of Ethical Dualism in International Affairs," and subsequently published it in the March 1993 edition of *Ethics and International Affairs*.

2. Reinhold Niebuhr, *Faith and Politics: A Commentary on Religious, Social and Political Thought in a Technological Age,* ed. Ronald H. Stone (N.Y.: George Braziller, 1968), 60-61. This originally appeared in 1957 in *The Ecumenical Review*.

3. Russell Foster Sizemore, "Reinhold Niebuhr and the Rhetoric of Liberal Anti-Communism: Christian Realism and the Rise of the Cold War," Ph.D. diss., Harvard University, 1987, 115.

4. Henry Kissinger, "Reflections on Containment," *Foreign Affairs* 73 (May/June 1994): 122.

5. Kissinger, "Reflections on Containment."

6. Niebuhr, *The Children of Light and the Children of Darkness: A Vindication of Democracy and a Critique of Its Traditional Defense* (N.Y.: Charles Scribner's Sons, 1966), 60.

7. Niebuhr, *The Children of Light and the Children of Darkness*, 63-64.

8. Niebuhr, *The Children of Light and the Children of Darkness*, 75-76.

9. Niebuhr, *The Children of Light and the Children of Darkness*, 82-83.

10. Reinhold Niebuhr, *A Reinhold Niebuhr Reader: Selected Essays, Articles, and Book Reviews,* ed. Charles C. Brown (Philadelphia: Trinity Press International, 1992), 96.

11. Niebuhr, *The Children of Light and the Children of Darkness*, 73-74.

12. This point is made by Niebuhr in his preface to Maurice Cranston's *What Are Human Rights?* (pp. vviii). In the preface Niebuhr writes approvingly of Cranston's view of human rights as moral law as distinct from positive law.

13. David Little, "The Recovery of Liberalism: *Moral Man and Immoral Society* Sixty Years Later" A paper delivered on February 25, 1992, at a conference on "Self-Interests and the Common Good: The Problem of Ethical Dualism in International Affairs," sponsored by the Carnegie Council on Ethics and International Affairs, University of Georgia, 38.

14. Reinhold Niebuhr, "Reply to Interpretation and Criticism," in *Reinhold Niebuhr: His Religious, Social and Political Thought* ed. Charles W. Kegley (N.Y.: The Pilgrim Press, 1984), 511.

15. Little, "The Recovery of Liberalism," 36.

16. Little, "The Recovery of Liberalism," 36.

17. Louis Henkin, "Rights: American and Human," *Columbia Law Review* 3 (April 1979) 408-10.

18. John J. Maresca, *To Helsinki: The Conference on Security and Cooperation in Europe 1973-1975* (Durham, N.C.: Duke University Press), xi.

19. William Korey, *The Promises We Keep: Human Rights, the Helsinki Process, and American Foreign Policy* (N.Y.: St. Martin's Press), xviii.

20. Michael Howard, "The World according to Henry: From Metternich to Me," *Foreign Affairs* 73 (May/June 1994): 133.

Selected Bibliography

Abrams, Ray H. *Preachers Present Arms: The Role of American Churches and Clergy in World* Wars *I and II, with Some Observations on the War in Vietnam.* Scottdale, Pa.: Herald Press, 1969.

Albrecht-Carrie, Rene. *A Diplomatic History of Europe since the Congress of Vienna.* N.Y.: Harper and Brothers Publishers, 1958.

Alexeyeva, Ludmilla. *Soviet Dissent: Contemporary Movements for National, Religious,and Human Rights.* Translated by Carol Pearce and John Glad. Middletown, Conn.: Wesleyan University Press, 1985.

American Baptist Churches in the U.S.A., "Policy Statement on Human Rights," adopted by the General Board of the American Baptist Churches, December 1976.

Aquinas, Thomas. *Treatise on Law (Summa Theologica, Questions 90-97).* With an introduction by Stanley Parry. Washington, D.C.: A Gateway Edition, Regnery Gateway, 1988.

Aristotle. *The Basic Works of Aristotle.* Edited and with an introduction by Richard McKeon. *Politics.* N.Y.: Random House, 1941.

"Background Memorandum for President Carter Regarding Concerns which Officers and Leaders of the National Council of Churches Want to Discuss with Him at Their Meeting February 24, 1978." In the National Council of Churches Washington Office Files.

Bastid, Suzanne. "The Special Significance of the Helsinki Final Act." In *Human Rights, International Law and the Helsinki Accord*. Edited by Thomas Buergenthal assisted by Judith R. Hall, 11-19. N.Y.: Allanheld, Osman Universe Books, 1977.

Beitz, Charles R. *Political Theory and International Relations*. Princeton, N.J.: Princeton University Press, 1979.

Bellah, Robert N. "Religious Influences on United States Foreign Policy." In *American Character and Foreign Policy*, ed. Michael P. Hamiliton, 50-60. Grand Rapids, Mich.: William B. Eerdmans Publishing Company, 1986.

Bennett, John C., and Harvey Seifert. *U.S. Foreign Policy and Christian Ethics*. Philadelphia: The Westminster Press, 1977.

Bentham, Jeremy. *The Works of Jeremy Bentham*. Published under the superintendence of his executor John Bowring. Vol. 2. "Anarchical Fallacies: Being an Examination of the Declaration of Rights Issued during the French Revolution." New York: Russell and Russell, Inc., 1962.

Beres, Louis Rene. *Reason and Realpolitik: U.S. Foreign Policy and World Order*. Lexington, Mass.: Lexington Books, D.C. Heath and Company, 1984.

Billingsly, Lloyd. *From Mainline to Sideline: The Social Witness of the National Council of Churches*. Washington, D.C.: Ethics and Public Policy Center, 1990.

Brill, Earl H. "Religious Influences on United States Foreign Policy." In American Character and Foreign Policy. Edited by Michael P. Hamilton, 60-66. Grand Rapids, Mich.: William B. Eerdmans Publishing Company, 1986.

Brown, Charles C. *Niebuhr and His Age: Reinhold Niebuhr's Prophetic Role in the Twentieth Century*. Philadelphia: Trinity Press International, 1992.

Brzezinski, Zbigniew. *Power and Principle: Memoirs of the National Security Adviser 1977-1981*. N.Y.: Farrar Straus and Giroux, 1983.

Buergenthal, Thomas. "Copenhagen: A Democratic Manifesto." *World Affairs* 153 (Summer 1990): 5-9.

___. "International Human Rights Law in the Helsinki Final Act: Conclusions." In *Human Rights, International Law and the Helsinki*

Accord. Edited by Thomas Buergenthal assisted by Judith R. Hall, 3-11. N.Y.: Allanheld, Osman Universe Books, 1977.

Bull, Hedley. "Society and Anarchy in International Relations." In *Conflict after the Cold War: Arguments on Causes of War and Peace.* Edited by Richard K. Betts, 136-149. N.Y.: Macmillan Publishing Company, 1994.

Cannon, Lou. *President Reagan: The Role of a Lifetime.* N.Y.: Simon and Schuster, 1991.

Carr, Edward Hallett. *The Twenty Years' Crisis 1919-1939: An Introduction to the Study of International Relations.* N.Y.: Harper Torchbooks, Harper and Row, 1964.

Carter, Jimmy. *Keeping Faith: Memoirs of a President.* N.Y. Bantam Books, 1982.

Carter, Stephen L. *The Culture of Disbelief: How American Law and Politics Trivialize Religious Devotion.* N.Y.: Basic Books, 1993.

Claude, Inis L. *Power and International Relations.* N.Y.: Random House, 1969.

Cobb, Charles E. "Report to Interunit Committee on International Concerns on The Working Committee of the Churches' Human Rights Programme for the Implementation of the Helsinki Final Act," January 13, 1984, from the files of the Washington Office of the National Council of Churches of Christ in the U.S.A.

Craig, Gordon A., and Alexander L. George. *Force and Statecraft: Diplomatic Problems of Our Time.* 2d ed. N.Y.: Oxford University Press, 1990.

Cranston, Maurice. "What Are Human Rights?" In *The Human Rights Reader.* Edited by Walter Laqueur and Barry Rubin, 17-25. N.Y.: New American Library, A Meridan Book, 1977.

___.*What Are Human Rights?* With a preface by Reinhold Niebuhr. N.Y.: Basic Books, Inc. 1962.

Dallek, Robert. *The American Style of Foreign Policy: Cultural Politics and Foreign Affairs.* N.Y.: Oxford University Press, 1983.

Drinan, Robert F. "Religion and the Future of Human Rights." *The Christian Century* (12-19 August 1987): 683-687.

Epps, Dwain C. to Congresswoman Millicent Fenwick, 1 June 1976. In files of the Washington Office of the National Council of Churches of Christ in the U.S.A.

Fascell, Dante B. "Did Human Rights Survive Belgrade?" *Foreign Policy* 31 (Summer 1978): 104-119.

Ferguson, C. Clyde. "Myres S. McDougal Distinguished Lecture Global Human Rights: Challenges and Prospects." *Denver Journal of International Law and Policy* 8 (Spring 1979): 367-379.

Formicola, Jo Renee. "The American Catholic Church and Its Role in the Formulation of United States Human Rights Foreign Policy 1945-1978." Ph.D. diss., Drew University, 1981.

Forsythe, David P. *Human Rights and World Politics*. 2d ed. Lincoln: University of Nebraska Press, 1989.

Frankel, Charles. *Human Rights and Foreign Policy*. Headline Series 241. N.Y.:Foreign Policy Association, 1978.

____."Morality and U.S. Foreign Policy." In *Private and Public Ethics: Tensions between Conscience and Institutional Responsibility*. Edited by Donald G. Jones, 62-96. N.Y.: The Edwin Mellen Press, 1978.

Frankena, William K. *Ethics*. 2d ed. Foundations of Philosophy Series. Englewood Cliffs, N. J.: Prentice-Hall, Inc. 1973.

Galey, Margaret E. "Congress, Foreign Policy and Human Rights Ten Years After Helsinki." *Human Rights: A Comparative and International Journal of the Social Sciences, Humanities, and Law* 3 (August 1985): 334-373.

Gewirth, Alan. *Human Rights: Essays on Justification and Applications*. Chicago: University of Chicago Press, 1982.

Good, Robert C. "The National Interest and Political Realism: Niebuhr's 'Debate' with Morgenthau and Kennan." *Journal of Politics* 22:4 (November 1960): 597-619.

Greenawalt, Kent. *Religious Convictions and Political Choice*. N.Y.: Oxford University Press, 1988.

Hamilton, Mr. Jim, Director of the National Council of Churches of Christ Washington Office. Telephone interview by author, 16 September 1996.

Hare, J. E. and Carey B. Joynt. *Ethics and International Affairs*. N.Y.: St. Martin's Press, 1982.

Hartz, Louis. *The Liberal Tradition in America: An Interpretation of American Political Thought since the Revolution*. With an Introduction by Tom Wicker. N.Y.: Harcourt Brace Jovanovich,

1991.

Hehir, J. Bryan. "Human Rights and U.S. Foreign Policy: A Perspective from Theological Ethics." In *The Moral Imperatives of Human Rights: A World Survey*. Edited by Kenneth W. Thompson, 1-25. N.Y.: University Press of America, 1980.

Hendrickson, David C. "The Renovation of American Foreign Policy." *Foreign Affairs* 71 (Spring 1992): 48-64.

Henkin, Louis. "Rights: American and Human." *Columbia Law Review* 3 (April 1979): 405-426.

___.*The Age of Rights*. N.Y.: Columbia University Press, 1990.

Herberg, Will. *Protestant-Catholic-Jew: An Essay in American Religious Sociology*. Garden City, N.Y.: Anchor Books Doubleday and Company, Inc., 1960.

Hertzke, Allen D. *Representing God in Washington: The Role of Religious Lobbies in the American Polity*. Knoxville: University of Tennessee Press, 1988.

Hoffmann, Stanley. *Duties beyond Borders: On the Limits and Possibilities of Ethical International Relations*. Syracuse, N.Y.: Syracuse University Press, 1988.

___.*Gulliver's Troubles, Or the Setting of American Foreign Policy*. A volume in the series "The Atlantic Policy Studies" published for the Council on Foreign Relations. N.Y.: McGraw-Hill Book Company, 1968.

Holleman, Warren Lee. *The Human Rights Movement: Western Values and Theological Perspectives*. N.Y.: Praeger, 1987.

Hooker, Richard. *Of the Laws of Ecclesiastical Polity: Preface, Book I and Book VIII*. Edited by Arthur Stephen McGrade. N.Y.: Cambridge University Press, 1994.

Howard, Michael. "The World according to Henry: From Metternich to Me." *Foreign Affairs* 73 (May/June 1994): 132-140.

Hudson, Winthrop S. *Religion in America: An Historical Account of the Development of American Religious Life*. 2d ed. N.Y.: Charles Scribner's Sons, 1973.

___. ed. *Nationalism and Religion in America: Concepts of American Identity and Mission*. N.Y.: Harper and Row, 1970.

Hutcheson, Richard G. Jr. *God in the White House: How Religion Has Changed the Modern Presidency*. N.Y.: Macmillan Publishing

Company, 1988.

Isaacson, Walter. *Kissinger: A Biography*. N.Y.: Simon and Schuster, 1992.

Johnson, M. Glen. "Historical Perspectives on Human Rights and U.S. Foreign Policy." *Universal Human Rights: A Comparative and International Journal of the Social Sciences, Philosophy and Law* 2 (July-September 1980): 1-18.

Kampelman, Max M. "Human Rights and Foreign Policy." In *Andrei Sakharov and Peace*. Edited by Edward D. Lozansky, 311-319. N.Y.: Avon, 1985.

____.*Entering New Worlds: The Memoirs of a Private Man in Public Life*. N.Y.: HarperCollins,1991.

Kant, Immanuel. *The Philosophy of Kant: Immanuel Kant's Moral and Political Writings*. Edited by Carl J. Friedrich. N.Y.: The Modern Library, 1977.

Kavass, Igor I., Jacqueline Poquin Granier, and Mary Francis Dominick, eds. *Human Rights, European Politics, and the Helsinki Accord: The Documentary Evolution of the Conference on Security and Co-operation in Europe 1973-1975*. Buffalo, N.Y.: William S. Hein and Co., Inc., 1981.

Kegley Jr., Charles W., ed. *Controversies in International Relations Theory: Realism and the Neoliberal Challenge*. N.Y.: St. Martin's Press, 1995.

Kennan, George F. "On American Principles." *Foreign Affairs* 74 (March/April 1995): 116-126.

____.*The Nuclear Delusion: Soviet-American Relations in the Atomic Age*. N.Y.: Pantheon Books,1982.

Kissinger, Henry A. Review of *Churchill: The Unruly Giant*, by Norman Rose. In *The N.Y. Times Book Review* 16, July 1995: 7.

____.*The White House Years*. Boston: Little, Brown and Company, 1979.

____."Reflections on Containment." *Foreign Affairs* 73 (May/June 1994): 113-132.

____.*Years of Upheaval*. Boston: Little, Brown and Company, 1982.

____."Continuity and Change in American Foreign Policy." In *Human Rights and World Order*. Edited by Abdul Aziz Said, 154-167. New Brunswick, N.J.: Transaction Books, 1978.

____.*Diplomacy*. N.Y.: Simon and Schuster, 1994.

Korey, William. *The Promises We Keep: Human Rights, the Helsinki Process, and American Foreign Policy.* With a foreword by Daniel Patrick Moynihan. N.Y.: St. Martin's Press, 1993.

___.*Human Rights and the Helsinki Accord: Focus on U.S. Policy.* Headline Series 264. N.Y.: Foreign Policy Association, 1983.

Leary, Virginia. "The Implementation of the Human Rights Provisions of the Helsinki Final Act A Preliminary Assessment: 1975-1977." In *Human Rights, International Law and the Helsinki Accord.* Edited by Thomas Buergenthal assisted by Judith R. Hall, 111-156. N.Y.: Allanheld, Osman Universe Books, 1977.

Lefever, Ernest W. "The Trivialization of Human Rights." *Policy Review* 3 (Winter 1978): 11-26.

___.*Ethics and United States Foreign Policy.* N.Y.: Meridian Books, Inc., 1957.

Lippy, Charles H., and Peter W. Williams, eds. *Encyclopedia of the American Religious Experience: Studies of Traditions and Movements.* N.Y.: Charles Scribner's Sons. S.v. "Civil and Public Religion," by Donald G. Jones.

Little, David. "The Recovery of Liberalism: *Moral Man and Immoral Society Sixty Years Later.*" A paper delivered February 25, 1992 at a conference on "Self-Interests and the Common Good: The Problem of Ethical Dualism in International Affairs." Sponsored by the Carnegie Council on Ethics and International Affairs, the University of Georgia.

Livezey, Lowell W. *Nongovernmental Organizations and the Ideas of Human Rights.* Publication of the Center for International Studies, World Order Studies Program Occasional Paper, no. 15. Princeton, N. J.: Princeton University Press, 1988.

___."U.S. Religious Organizations and the International Human Rights Movement." *Human Rights Quarterly: A Comparative and International Journal of the Social Sciences, Humanities, and Law* 11 (February 1989):14-82.

Locke, John. *Two Treatises of Government.* A critical edition with an introduction by Peter Laslett. N.Y.: The New American Library, 1965.

Lossky, Nicholas, Jose Miguez Bonino, John Pobee, Tom Stransky,Geoffrey Wainwright, and Pauline Webb, eds. *Dictionary of the Ecumenical Movement.* Grand Rapids, Mich.: William B. Eerdmans Publishing Company, WCC Publications, 1991. S.v. "Human Rights," by Erich Weingartner.

Lovin, Robin W. "Niebuhr at 100: Realism for New Realities." *The Christian Century* 109 (June 17-24, 1992): 604-5.

___.*Reinhold Niebuhr and Christian Realism.* Cambridge, U.K.: Cambridge University Press, 1995.

___."Re-examining Human Rights." *The Christian Century* (August 26 - September 2, 1981): 829-833.

Maresca, John J. *To Helsinki: The Conference on Security and Cooperation in Europe 1973-1975.* New edition. With a foreword by William E. Griffith. Durham, N.C.: Duke University Press, 1987.

Maritan, Jacques. *The Rights of Man and Natural Law.* Translated by Doris C. Anson. N.Y.: Charles Scribner's Sons, 1943.

Martin, Rex. "Human Rights and Civil Rights." In *The Philosophy of Human Rights*, Morton E. Winston, 75-86. Belmont, Calif.: Wadsworth Publishing Company, 1989.

May, Ernest R. *American Imperialism: A Speculative Essay.* N.Y.: Atheneum, 1968.

May, Henry F. *The Divided Heart: Essays on Protestantism and the Enlightenment in America.* N.Y.: Oxford University Press, 1991.

McCann, Dennis. *Christian Realism and Liberation Theology: Practical Theologies in Creative Conflict.* Maryknoll, N.Y.: Orbis Books, 1982.

McCurley, Foster R. and John H. Reumann. "Human Rights in the Law and Romans (Series A)." In Human Rights: Rhetoric or Reality. Edited by George W. Forell and William H. Lazareth, 17-31. Philadelphia: Fortress Press, 1978.

McElroy, Robert W. *Morality and American Foreign Policy: The Role of Ethics in International Affairs.* Princeton, N.J.: Princeton University Press, 1992.

McNeill, John T. "Natural Law in the Teaching of the Reformers." *The Journal of Religion* 26 (July 1946): 168-183.

Mead, Sidney E. *The Nation with the Soul of a Church.* N.Y.: Harper and Row, Publishers, 1975.

Merk, Frederick, and Lois Bannister Merk. *Manifest Destiny and Missions in American History: A Reinterpretation.* N.Y.: Alfred A. Knopf.

Meyer, Peter. "The International Bill: A Brief History." In *The International Bill of Human Rights.* XXIII-XLVII. With a foreword by Jimmy Carter. With an afterword by Adolfo Perez Esquivel. With an introduction by Tom J. Farer. Glen Ellen, Calif.: Entwhistle Books, 1981.

Morgenthau, Hans. "The Present Tragedy of America." *Worldview* 12 (September 1969): 14-15.

Morgenthau, Hans, and Kenneth W. Thompson. *Politics among Nations: The Struggle for Power and Peace.* 6th Edited by N.Y.: McGraw-Hill Publishing Company, 1985.

___.*Scientific Man vs. Power Politics.* Chicago: University of Chicago Press, 1946; reprint, Chicago: University of Chicago Press, 1974.

___."National Interest and Moral Principles in Foreign Policy: The Primacy of the National Interest." *American Scholar* XVIII (Spring 1949). Quoted in Robert C. Good. "The National Interest and Political Realism: Niebuhr's 'Debate' with Morgenthau and Kennan." *Journal of Politics* 22 (November 1960), 597-619.

Mott, Stephen Charles. "The Contribution of the Bible to Human Rights." Chapter in *Human Rights and the Global Mission of the Church,* 5-13. Cambridge, Mass.: Boston Theological Institute, 1985.

Muravchik, Joshua. *The Uncertain Crusade: Jimmy Carter and the Dilemmas of Human Rights Policy.* With a foreword by Jeane Kirkpatrick. N.Y.: Hamilton Press, 1981.

Myrdal, Gunnar with the assistance of Richard Sterner and Arnold Rose. *An American Dilemma: The Negro Problem and Modern Democracy.* Twentieth Anniversary Edition. N.Y.: Harper and Row, Publishers, 1962.

Nardin, Terry, and David R. Mapel, eds. *Traditions of International Ethics.* Cambridge, England: Cambridge University Press, 1992.

Neuhaus, Richard John. *The Naked Public Square: Religion and Democracy in America.* 2d Edited by Grand Rapids, Mich.: William B. Eerdmans Publishing Company, 1984.

Newman, Jeremiah. *Conscience versus Law: Reflections on the Evolution of Natural Law.* Chicago: Franciscan Herald Press, 1971.

Niebuhr, Reinhold. "The Social Myths of the 'Cold War.'" *Journal of International Affairs* 21 (1967): 40-56.

___.*An Interpretation of Christian Ethics*. N.Y.: Harper and Brothers, 1935. Reprint. N.Y.: The Seabury Press, A Crossroad Book, 1979.

___.*Faith and Politics: A Commentary on Religious, Social and Political Thought in a Technological Age*. Edited by Ronald H. Stone. N.Y.: George Braziller, 1968.

___.*Christian Realism and Political Problems*. N.Y.: Charles Scribner's Sons, 1953.

___.*The Children of Light and the Children of Darkness: A Vindication of Democracy and a Critique of Its Traditional Defense*. N.Y.: Charles Scribner's Sons, 1966.

___.*Christianity and Power Politics*. N.Y.: Charles Scribner's Sons, 1940. Reprint, N.Y.: Archon Books, 1969.

___.*Moral Man and Immoral Society: A Study in Ethics and Politics*. New York: Charles Scribner's Sons, 1960.

___.*The Nature and Destiny of Man*. Vol. 2, *Human Destiny*. N.Y.: Charles Scribner's Sons, 1943.

___."Reply to Interpretation and Criticism." In Reinhold Niebuhr: His Religious, Social and Political Thought, Edited by Charles W. Kegley, 507-527. N.Y.: The Pilgrim Press, 1984.

___.*Reinhold Niebuhr: Theologian of Public Life*. Edited by Larry Rasmussen. In *The Making of Modern Theology*, general editor John de Gruchy. London: Collins, 1988.

___.*Faith and History: A Comparison of Christian and Modern Views of History*. N.Y.: Charles Scribner's Sons, Macmillan Publishing Company, 1949.

___.*The Structure of Nations and Empires: A Study of the Recurring Patterns and Problems of the Political Order in Relation to the Unique Problems of the Nuclear Age*. N.Y.: Charles Scribner's Sons, 1959.

___."Must We Do Nothing?" In *The Christian Century Reader: Representative Articles, Editorials, and Poems Selected from More than Fifty Years of the Christian Century*. Edited by Harold E. Fey and Margaret Frakes, 222-228. N.Y.: Association Press, 1962.

___.*The Essential Reinhold Niebuhr*. Edited and with an introduction by Robert McAfee Brown. New Haven, Conn.: Yale University Press, 1986.

___.*A Reinhold Niebuhr Reader: Selected Essays,Articles, and Book Reviews*. Edited by Charles C. Brown. Philadelphia: Trinity Press International, 1992.

___.*Love and Justice: Selections from the Shorter Writings of Reinhold Niebuhr*. Edited by D. B. Robertson. Louisville, Ky.: Westminster/John Knox Press, 1957.

Novak, Michael. *Taking Glasnost Seriously: Toward an Open Soviet Union*. Washington, D.C.: American Enterprise Institute for Public Policy Research, 1988.

Nye, Joseph S. Jr. *Nuclear Ethics*. N.Y.: The Free Press, 1980.

O'Dea, Thomas F. *The Sociology of Religion*. Foundations of Modern Sociology Series. Englewood Cliffs, N. J.: Prentice-Hall, Inc., 1966.

Paton, David M., Edited by *Breaking Barriers Nairobi 1975: The Official Report of the Fifth Assembly of the World Council of Churches*, Nairobi, 23 November-10 December, 1975. Grand Rapids, Mich.: William B. Eerdmans, 1976.

Perry, Michael J. *Love and Power: The Role of Religion and Morality in American Politics*. N.Y.: Oxford University Press, 1991.

Ramsey, Paul. *Who Speaks for the Church?: A Critique of the 1966 Geneva Conference on Church and Society*. N.Y.: Abingdon Press, 1967.

Randall, Claire. Testimony before the Senate Foreign Relations Committee, 21 January 1976 from the files of the Washington Office of the National Council of Churches of Christ in the U.S.A.

___.General Secretary of the National Council of Churches of Christ in the U.S.A. Telephone interview by author, 1 November 1996.

Richey, Russell E., and Donald G. Jones. *American Civil Religion*. N.Y.: Harper and Row, 1974.

Rosenthal, Joel H. *Righteous Realists: Political Realism, Responsible Power, and American Culture in the Nuclear Age*. Baton Rouge: Louisiana State University Press, 1991.

Sabine, George H. *A History of Political Theory*. 3d Edited by N.Y.: Holt, Rinehart and Winston, 1961.

Sharansky, Natan. *Fear No Evil.* Translated by Stefani Hoffman. N.Y.: Random House, 1988.

Shinn, Roger L. "Realism and Ethics in Political Philosophy." In *A Tribute to Hans Morgenthau.* With an intellectual autobiography by Hans J. Morgenthau. Edited by Kenneth Thompson and Robert J. Myers with the assistance of Robert Osgood and Tang Tsou, 95-104. Washington, D.C.: The New Republic Book Company, Inc., 1977.

Sizemore, Russell Foster. "Reinhold Niebuhr and the Rhetoric of Liberal Anti- Communism: Christian Realism and the Rise of the Cold War." Ph.D. diss., Harvard University, 1987.

Smith, Gaddis. *Morality, Reason, and Power: American Diplomacy in the Carter Years.* N.Y.: Hill and Wang, 1986.

Smith, Hedrick. *The New Russians.* N.Y.: Avon Books, 1991.

Stackhouse, Max L. *Creeds, Society, and Human Rights: A Study in Three Cultures.* Grand Rapids, Mich.: William B. Eerdmans Publishing Company, 1984.

____."Public Theology, Human Rights and Missions." In *Human Rights and the Global Mission of the Church.* 13-22. Cambridge, Mass.: Boston Theological Institute, 1985.

Stassen, Harold. *The Stassen Draft Charter for a New United Nations 1985.* Philadelphia: The Glenview Foundation. Revised October 24, 1985.

Stoessinger, John G. *Crusaders and Pragmatists: Movers of Modern American Foreign Policy.* 2d ed. N.Y.: Norton and Company, 1985.

____.*Nations in Darkness: China, Russia, and America.* 5th ed. N.Y.: McGraw-Hill Publishing Company, 1990.

Stone, Ronald H. *Christian Realism and Peacemaking: Issues in U.S. Foreign Policy.* Nashville: Abingdon Press, 1988.

____.*Professor Reinhold Niebuhr: A Mentor to the Twentieth Century.* Louisville, Ky.: Westminster/John Knox Press, 1973.

Szabo, Imre. "Historical Foundations of Human Rights and Subsequent Developments." In *The International Dimensions of Human Rights.* Vol. 1. 11-43. General editor Karel Vasak. Revised and edited for English edition by Philip Alston. Westport, Conn.: Greenwood Press, 1982.

Thompson, Kenneth W. *Traditions and Values in Politics and Diplomacy: Theory and Practice*. Baton Rouge: Louisana State University Press, 1992.

___.*Christian Ethics and the Dilemmas of Foreign Policy*. Durham, N.C.: Duke University Press, 1959.

Traer, Robert. *Faith in Human Rights: Support in Religious Traditions for a Global Struggle*. Washington, D.C.: Georgetown University Press, 1991.

Troeltsch, Ernst. *The Social Teaching of the Christian Churches*. Translated by Olive Wyon. With an introduction by H. Richard Niebuhr. Chicago: University of Chicago Press, 1981.

Twiss, Sumner B., and Bruce Grelle. "Human Rights and Comparative Religious Ethics: A New Venue." In *The Annual of the Society of Christian Ethics 1995*, 21-49. Boston, Mass.: The Society of Christian Ethics, 1995.

U.S. President. *Public Papers of the Presidents of the United States*. Washington, D.C. Office of the Federal Register, National Archives and Records Service, 1973-1981. Richard M. Nixon, Gerald R. Ford, Jimmy Carter.

U.S. Congress. House. Committee on Foreign Affairs. Subcommittee on International Organization and Movements. *Human Rights in the World Community: A Call for U.S. Leadership*. 93rd Cong., 2d sess., 1974.

U.S. Congress. House. Committee on International Relations. *Conference on Security and Cooperation in Europe: Part II, Hearings before the Subcommittee on International Political and Military Affairs of the Committee on International Relations*. 94th Cong., 2d Sess., 4 May 1976.

U.S. Congress. Senate. Committee on Foreign Relations. *International Human Rights Treaties: Hearings before the Committee on Foreign Relations*. 96th Cong., 1st Sess., 14, 15, 16, 19 November 1979.

U.S. Congress. House. Committee on International Relations. Subcommittee on International Organizations. *Human Rights and United States Foreign Policy: A Review of the Administration's Record*. 95th Cong., 1st sess., 1977.

U.S. Congress. House. Committee on International Relations. *Conference on Security and Cooperation in Europe: Hearing before the*

Subcommittee on International Political and Military Affairs of the Committee on International Relations. 94th Cong., 1st Sess., 6 May 1975.

U.S. Department of State. Bureau of Public Affairs. "Conference on Security and Cooperation in Europe: Final Act, Helsinki, 1975." *Bulletin Reprint* from *The Department of State Bulletin*, 1 September 1975.

Ulam, Adam B. *Dangerous Relations: The Soviet Union in World Politics, 1970-1982.* N.Y.: Oxford University Press, 1983.

Vance, Cyrus. *Hard Choices: Critical Years in America's Foreign Policy.* N.Y. Simon and Schuster, 1983.

Von Glahn, Gerhard. *Law among Nations: An Introduction to Public International Law.* 6th ed. N.Y.: Macmillan Publishing Company, 1992.

Wald, Kenneth D. *Religion and Politics in the United States.* 2d Edited by Washington, D.C.: CQ Press, 1992.

Wimer, Ms. Alice, director of International Affairs of the National Council of Churches of Christ in the U.S.A. Telephone interview by author, 28 September 1995.

Wilson, Woodrow. *The Public Papers of Woodrow Wilson, War and Peace.* Vol. II. Edited by Ray S. Baker and William E. Dodd. N.Y.: Harper, 1927. Quoted in Inis Claude. *Power and International Relations,* 82, n. 1. N.Y.: Random House, 1969.

Winston, Morton E. *The Philosophy of Human Rights.* Belmont, Calif.: Wadsworth Publishing Company, 1989.

Wiseberg, Laurie S., and Harry M. Scoble. "Recent Trends in the Expanding Universe of Nongovernmental Organizations Dedicated to the Protection of Human Rights." *Denver Journal of International Law and Policy 8* (Special Issue 1979): 627-659.

Wolfers, Arnold. *Discord and Collaboration: Essays on International Politics.* Foreword by Reinhold Niebuhr. Baltimore: Johns Hopkins University Press, 1962.

Index

About the Author

L. Larry Pullen is visiting assistant professor of political science at Eastern College. Born in Charleston, West Virginia, he attended Marshall University in Huntington, West Virginia, and received his B.A. from West Virginia University in 1969, and his Ph.D. from Drew University in 1997. In addition he holds the Master of Divinity degree from Colgate Rochester Divinity School - Bexley Hall - Crozer Theological Seminary and the Master of International Service degree from the American University's School of International Service. Before coming to Eastern College, he taught at Alvernia College. Pullen served as Director of the Peace Concerns Program of the American Baptist Churches from 1980 to 1986. He lives in West Chester, Pennsylvania, with his wife and two daughters.